THE BRIDGE WORLD
39 WEST 94th STREET
NEW YORK, N. Y. 10025

The
Daily Telegraph
Bridge Quiz

G.C.H. Fox has also written

Modern Bidding Systems in Bridge
Bridge: Standard Bidding
Begin Bridge
The Daily Telegraph Book of Bridge
Master Play: The Best of International Bridge

The
Daily Telegraph
Bridge Quiz

G. C. H. FOX

ROBERT HALE · LONDON

© *The Daily Telegraph* and G.C.H. Fox 1977
First published in Great Britain 1977

ISBN 0 7091 6148 4

Robert Hale Limited
Clerkenwell House
Clerkenwell Green
London EC1R OHT

Photoset by
Specialised Offset Services Ltd, Liverpool
Printed in Great Britain by
Lowe & Brydone Ltd.,
Thetford, Norfolk

Preface

The annual *Daily Telegraph* Christmas bridge quiz competition, the problems of which I have enjoyed setting for many years, has always been a popular feature attracting numerous entries from a wide range of enthusiastic players. The prizes offered are modest and cannot possibly account for the competition's popularity which I suspect is due to a basic desire to test one's skill and ability. Some competitors send in concise answers whilst others write pages and pages with the most exhaustive analyses.

I welcomed the suggestion that a selection of problems from these competitions should appear in a more permanent form and took the opportunity to enlarge on explanations which originally could only be given in brief terms. The established format of dividing questions into Bidding, Leading, Defence and Declarer Play has been retained.

It is hoped this Quiz Book will prove both interesting and instructive to all players ranging from the average to the near expert. The newly introduced rating tables will enable the reader to assess his abilities and highlight areas requiring attention.

G.C.H. FOX

Rate Your Game

Max 300	Bidding (*page 9*)
250-300	Inspired. You only have to match it with your play to be a world beater.
150-250	Above average. A reliable bidding partner.
150-below	Not so good. You will need to play very well to make some of the curious contracts you may reach.

Max 100	Leading (*page 31*)
75-100	You should always arrange to be on lead when your side is defending.
50-75	Above average. You will not give many tricks away on the lead.
50-below	Maybe you are just unlucky. Your best chance is to buy the contracts or hope your partner leads.

Max 300	Defence (*page 45*)
250-300	Very good indeed. Opponents will realise they cannot afford to overbid against you.
150-250	Above average. Clearly you are a competent defender.
150-below	Much room for improvement. Maybe you are better as declarer?

Max 300	Declarer Play (*page 75*)
250-300	Excellent. You can well afford to bid boldly.
150-200	Above average. You will not lose many contracts that are there.
150-below	Considerable scope for improvement – perhaps defence is your *forte*?

Part 1
Bidding

Bidding

The questions on bidding are based on a modern form of standard British style method, consistent with either Two Clubs System or Acol. Opening bids in no-trumps are assumed to be 12-14 points non-vulnerable, 15-17 points vulnerable, with the Stayman Convention to investigate a four card major suit. Opening bids of three and higher are normal pre-emptive calls and Blackwood is used for slams. Unless otherwise stated all problems relate to rubber bridge.

1. You are South, dealer, with East-West vulnerable. What do you say on each of the following?

   (a) ♠ A J 9 6   ♥ K Q 10 7   ♦ Q 10 6   ♣ A 10

   (b) ♠ A   ♥ A K 10 9 5 3   ♦ A K 8 6 5   ♣ 3

   (c) ♠ Q 9 6 4 2   ♥ A 9 2   ♦ K 5 2   ♣ Q 3

   (d) ♠ K Q J 9 8 7 4   ♥ A 5   ♦ 3 2   ♣ 8 7

   (e) ♠ Q J 10 9 8 6 4 2   ♥ –   ♦ A K Q J 10   ♣ –

   (f) ♠ K Q 10 8   ♥ K 3   ♦ Q 10 6   ♣ K J 10 9

2. You are South. North, your partner, deals and opens one no-trump (12-14) and East passes. What do you say on each of the following?

    (a) ♠J96432 ♡54 ◇1086 ♣74

    (b) ♠108642 ♡Q762 ◇86 ♣75

    (c) ♠74 ♡J43 ◇AKQ10754 ♣Q

    (d) ♠AQ1086 ♡96 ◇AJ6 ♣KJ9

    (e) ♠K1086 ♡K954 ◇Q62 ♣J5

    (f) ♠A62 ♡KQ9 ◇A864 ♣AJ2

3. You are South, with North dealer, and East-West vulnerable, playing duplicate pairs (match points). North opens three spades and East passes. What do you say on each of the following?

    (a) ♠J2 ♡AJ42 ◇KJ62 ♣QJ6

    (b) ♠3 ♡AK985 ◇A106 ♣KQ96

    (c) ♠Q643 ♡53 ◇KQ1064 ♣74

    (d) ♠A96 ♡KJ2 ◇AQ6 ♣KJ98

    (e) ♠AJ ♡A ◇AKQJ754 ♣A43

    (f) ♠– ♡QJ43 ◇KQ9862 ♣A63

4. You are South with East-West vulnerable. North deals and opens one heart and East overcalls with one spade. What do you say on each of the following?

(a) ♠ 4 2   ♡ J 9 8 5   ◇ K 8 6 4   ♣ Q 7 5

(b) ♠ K J 9 8 5   ♡ 2   ◇ A J 4   ♣ Q 10 7 5

(c) ♠ K 10 6   ♡ J 3   ◇ K 9 8 4   ♣ J 9 7 3

(d) ♠ A   ♡ K 7 3   ◇ A K J 9 4 3   ♣ K 6 2

(e) ♠ Q 10 8 6 4 2   ♡ 5 4   ◇ J 6 2   ♣ 10 3

(f) ♠ 4 2   ♡ Q 9 6   ◇ K J 9 7 6   ♣ J 5 3

5. You are South with both sides vulnerable. Your partner, North, deals and opens two clubs and rebids two no-trump after your negative reply of two diamonds, thereby showing a balanced hand with 23-24 high card points. What do you say on each of the following?

(a) ♠ Q 10 8 2   ♡ 6 2   ◇ K J 7 5   ♣ 5 3 2

(b) ♠ 7   ♡ K Q J 10 9 8   ◇ J 7 2   ♣ 9 8 3

(c) ♠ 4 3   ♡ Q 10 9 8 6 4   ◇ 10 9   ♣ J 5 3

(d) ♠ J 3 2   ♡ 9 6 4   ◇ 9 7 6 2   ♣ 7 5 3

(e) ♠ 4 2   ♡ 8 7 2   ◇ 5 4 3   ♣ K J 8 7 6

(f) ♠ J 6 4 2   ♡ K 9 7 6 2   ◇ Q 8 3   ♣ 2

6. You are South at love all. Your partner deals and opens one club and East passes. What do you say on each of the following?

   (a) ♠ K 6 2 ♡ Q 9 7 ◇ J 8 6 ♣ K 6 4 2

   (b) ♠ K 4 ♡ K 10 6 5 ◇ K 10 7 4 ♣ J 4 2

   (c) ♠ K 2 ♡ Q 10 6 ◇ A 10 2 ♣ A J 10 7 6

   (d) ♠ Q 4 2 ♡ 9 6 5 3 ◇ Q 6 3 2 ♣ 6 3

   (e) ♠ A K Q J 7 6 5 ♡ 4 2 ◇ K Q ♣ K 10

   (f) ♠ 2 ♡ A Q J 10 7 6 4 ◇ 10 8 ♣ Q J 2

7. You are South, dealer at love all, and open one heart. West passes and North responds two no-trump. East passes. What do you say on each of the following?

   (a) ♠ Q 5 2 ♡ A K J 7 2 ◇ K 2 ♣ Q 6 2

   (b) ♠ A J 4 2 ♡ A Q 10 8 4 ◇ 3 ♣ K 5 4

   (c) ♠ 7 3 2 ♡ K J 10 8 6 4 ◇ A 2 ♣ Q 10

   (d) ♠ K 4 2 ♡ A Q J 9 ◇ A Q 3 ♣ K 9 8

   (e) ♠ 3 2 ♡ A J 10 6 4 ◇ K J 9 8 ♣ A 6

   (f) ♠ 10 9 ♡ A Q 10 7 6 4 ◇ A Q 3 ♣ K 5

8. You are South with East-West vulnerable playing duplicate pairs (match points). East opens one heart. As South, what do you say on each of the following?

(a) ♠J 2 ♡A 2 ◇A K Q 10 5 3 2 ♣4 3

(b) ♠10 6 4 ♡K J 10 7 6 ◇K J 2 ♣K 4

(c) ♠K Q J 10 9 7 6 ♡3 ◇Q J 10 8 ♣6

(d) ♠A 10 8 3 ♡3 2 ◇A Q 7 4 3 ♣K 8

(e) ♠A Q J 9 8 ♡4 3 ◇7 6 4 ♣8 7 6

(f) ♠K 3 ♡K 10 8 6 ◇K J 9 6 4 ♣A 8

9. You are South, with North-South vulnerable. West deals and opens one diamond and North doubles. East bids one spade. As South what do you say on each of the following?

(a) ♠6 2 ♡K 8 6 ◇Q J 8 5 ♣Q 8 4 2

(b) ♠Q 10 7 5 2 ♡4 3 2 ◇7 2 ♣A 9 8

(c) ♠8 6 ♡J ◇K J 10 ♣A K Q 10 6 4 2

(d) ♠K J 2 ♡A J 4 2 ◇6 4 ♣K 10 8 4

(e) ♠3 2 ♡K J 10 8 6 4 3 ◇6 ♣A J 6

(f) ♠Q 2 ♡K J 8 2 ◇7 4 3 ♣Q 10 7 2

10. You are South and your side only is vulnerable. North, your partner, deals and opens one no-trump (15-17) and East overcalls with two diamonds (a natural bid, not conventional). As South what do you say on each of the following?

(a) ♠ Q 10 8 6 4 2 ♡ 3 2 ◇ 6 4 ♣ Q 6 3

(b) ♠ K 4 2 ♡ A Q J 7 6 ◇ 3 2 ♣ K 6 4

(c) ♠ K J 7 6 ♡ A Q 9 8 ◇ 6 5 ♣ Q J 7

(d) ♠ K 4 ♡ Q 10 8 ◇ K 10 8 7 ♣ J 6 4 2

(e) ♠ J 5 ♡ Q 6 4 ◇ J 3 ♣ A K Q J 5 4

(f) ♠ K 3 ♡ Q J 10 9 7 6 4 ◇ 2 ♣ Q J 3

Answers

	MAX. AWARD	YOUR SCORE
1(a) One heart = 5 points. One spade = 3 points.	5	

1(a) One heart = 5 points. One spade = 3 points.
The normal practice with two touching suits of equal length is to bid the higher ranking suit first. But with hands containing four cards in each major and 15+ high-card points the more modern practice is to open one heart, prepared to rebid two no-trump if partner responds two clubs or two diamonds, and to support him if he calls one spade. If one spade is opened and partner replies two clubs or two diamonds you cannot indicate your second suit with two hearts and at the same time show the all round quality of the hand with two no-trump.

(b) Two clubs = 5 points. Two hearts = 3 points.
The standard requirements for an opening bid of two clubs are either: (1) a balanced hand containing 23 or more high-card points, or (2) a hand containing five high-card tricks and which has a reasonable expectation of taking at least nine tricks. In other words, a hand with game-going potential regardless of the degree of support that partner may provide.

The present hand fulfils these requirements as some sort of fit in either hearts or diamonds will produce game. The late M. Harrison Gray, one of the four originators of the Acol System, opened this hand two clubs in the London County Masters Individual Championship.

c/f

| | 5 | |
| | 10 | |

	MAX. AWARD	YOUR SCORE
b/f	10	

1(c) No bid
It is permissible to open with 11 high-card points, but only with a good five-card suit. This has no substance.

| | 5 | |

(d) One spade.
Without the ace of hearts you would open three spades. As it is the hand is too strong.

| | 5 | |

(e) Five spades = 5 points. Two spades = 2 points. Four spades = 1 point.
A specialised bid. Partner should only raise holding top honours in spades (king and ace). Top cards in hearts and clubs are of no interest.

| | 5 | |

(f) One club = 5 points. One no-trump = 1 point.
Hands with four cards in clubs and spades should be opened one club even though, in points, they qualify for one no-trump. In the present case with three tens the hand is too strong for one no-trump as it is nearer to being 15 points than 14.

| | 5 | |

2(a) Two spades.
A simple example of the weak take-out. The hand is useless in no-trumps but has some value if spades are trumps. Partner is bound to hold at least two spades. Your reply is a complete sign-off and opener must pass. Two spades is also pre-emptive.

| | 5 | |

| c/f | 35 | |

	MAX. AWARD	YOUR SCORE
b/f	35	

2(b) Two clubs = 5 points. Two spades = 2 points. No Bid = 1 point. — **5**

The Stayman reply two clubs asking for a four card major suit is justified as you can always retreat to two spades if opener bids two diamonds denying four cards in either spades or hearts. If he replies two spades or two hearts you will pass, happy to have found a better contract than one no-trump. Using Stayman gives you two chances of finding a fit, as against one if you bid a direct two spades. Partner might have two spades and four hearts.

(c) Three no-trump. — **5**

A reasonable gamble. Provided your partner can get in in time he will make seven tricks out of nine with your diamonds. Pointless to call three diamonds, hoping he bids three no-trump.

(d) Three spades. — **5**

Jump bid and forcing to game. There is no point in using Stayman as you only require three-card support for your suit. A direct three no-trump would risk the loss of hearts. Players using transfer bids can count 5 points for a response of two hearts, requesting opener to transfer to two spades, enabling the no-trump hand to remain concealed.

(e) No Bid. — **5**

It may be tempting to bid two clubs (Stayman) hoping to find partner with a four-card major, but you cannot find a safe reply to two diamonds, denying four hearts or spades. It is a basic principle that when you use Stayman you must: (1) Be interested in playing the hand in a major suit as an alternative to no-trumps. (2) Be in a position to safeguard the final contract.

c/f	55	

	MAX. AWARD	YOUR SCORE
b/f	**55**	
	5	
	5	
	5	
	5	
	5	
c/f	**80**	

2(f) Three no-trump
   The maximum combined count is 32 and with no long suit a slam is unlikely.

3(a) No Bid.
   Opposite an opening bid of three you require three-four quick tricks. Here you hope to have enough for the contract to be made.

(b) Four spades = 5 points. No Bid = 1 point.
   Here you have four quick tricks and the best course is to raise partner in his suit, despite having a singleton. You can assume he holds at least seven. It would be wrong to bid three no-trump as you will not be able to make use of his suit and there is no point in bidding hearts as your partner is almost certainly short in that suit.

(c) Four spades = 5 points. Five spades = 3 points. No Bid = 2 points. Six spades = 1 point.
   As you have no defensive values apart from a possible trick in diamonds you should raise the bid to make it more difficult for the next player to take action. Of course you do not expect to make four spades but the penalty will almost certainly be less than the score opponents would be likely to make if they were allowed to get into the bidding cheaply. Here points are given for five spades and six spades as these bids might well prove effective. To pass is to take the line of least resistance and display a lack of enterprise.

(d) Three no-trump = 5 points. Four spades = 4 points.
   With a good fit in spades and with the lead coming up to your hand, nine tricks may well prove to be possible while four tricks might easily be lost in spades.

	MAX. AWARD	YOUR SCORE
b/f	**80**	

3(e) Five no-trump = 5 points. Six spades = 3 points. Four spades = 1 point.
> The grand slam force (five no-trump) asks partner to bid seven in the agreed suit (spades) if he holds two out of the three top honours in the suit. If you wanted to ask for kings you would first bid four no-trump and follow up with five no-trump. A direct bid of six spades is likely to succeed but there is little to gain by bidding diamonds.

5

(f) No Bid.
> Not a suitable hand for your partner but you will only make things worse by bidding.

5

4(a) Two hearts.
> A single raise of partner's suit after an intervening bid does not show additional values. You would have raised one heart to two hearts had West passed so there is no reason not to do so now. Consider what happens if you pass. East may support to two spades and your partner can scarcely continue single handed and you have surrendered the initiative. If you bid two hearts and the next player says two spades your partner may be able to push on to three hearts which may make, force the opponents up to three spades which may go down, or go down 50-100 playing in three hearts which is better than allowing the other side to make a part score.

5

(b) Double (Penalty double).

5

(c) One no-trump.
> This shows 8-10 points after an intervening bid and includes a stopper in opponent's suit.

5

c/f	**105**	

	MAX. AWARD	YOUR SCORE
b/f	**105**	

4(d) Three diamonds = 5 points. Two spades = 3 points.

    It is best to make a forcing to game jump to three diamonds and show your suit. You can indicate your first round control in spades later.

5

(e) No Bid.

    It would be wrong to double as you cannot contribute anything to the defence of an alternative contract.

5

(f) Two hearts = 5 points. No Bid = 1 point.

    Similar argument to (a) above; although you have here only three trumps you are light in high cards for two diamonds.

5

5(a) Three clubs = 5 points. Three no-trump = 3 points.

    Three clubs is Stayman asking partner to bid a four card major suit. In the sequence the rebid of two no-trump is merely an outsize two no-trump opening. You intend to raise three spades to four spades or bid three no-trump over any other reply. Those who favour the Baron use of three clubs, asking for four card suits in ascending order will be unaffected if partner bid three spades but will call three spades if opener bids three diamonds or three hearts.

5

(b) Four hearts = 5 points. Three hearts = 3 points. Three no-trump = 1 point.

    A jump bid after a negative reply shows a solid suit missing one top honour.

5

c/f	**130**	

	MAX. AWARD	YOUR SCORE
b/f	**130**	

5(c) Three hearts = 5 points. Three diamonds (Flint Convention) = 5 points. Four hearts = 3 points. **5**

You intend to rebid 4 hearts over three no-trump. The Flint Convention employs a reply of three diamonds and opener is obliged to reply three hearts. If the responder has a long and useless heart suit he can pass. If his suit is spades he converts to three spades. It is also possible to employ the three diamonds reply on better hands, intending to raise partner's hearts to four so that the strong hand remains concealed. A direct four hearts should not imply slam interest.

(d) No Bid. **5**

The opening bid is limited to 23-24 points so game is most unlikely.

(e) Three no-trump. **5**

There is no point at all in bidding three clubs. For one thing it would be Stayman and for another you do not want to play in five clubs. Your best chance of game is three no-trump so just bid it.

(f) Three clubs. **5**

Either Stayman or Baron. Those playing the Baron version may get into difficulties if opener rebids three diamonds (four diamonds) and you bid three hearts. Not knowing you hold a five card suit he will probably bid three no-trump unless he has four spades. You may now be in the wrong contract. Using Stayman you can bid three hearts after a rebid of three diamonds and this must show five hearts and, by inference, four spades, as you would not bid a four-card heart suit when your partner has no four card major.

c/f	**150**	

	MAX. AWARD	YOUR SCORE
b/f	**150**	

6(a) One no-trump = 5 points. Two clubs = 3 points.

    A response of one no-trump to one club generally implies about 8-9, possibly 10 points as it has by-passed cheaper bids in a suit. A raise to two clubs is not completely wrong and a temporizing bid, such as one diamond, might work out alright. It is not, of course, any form of denial.

    5

(b) One heart = 5 points. One diamond = 3 points. One no-trump = 1 point.

    It's usual when responding with two four card suits to bid the cheaper so one diamond might seem to be right, but with four cards each in diamonds and hearts the modern practice is to bid one heart, as an intervening bid of one spade over one diamond may make it difficult to find a heart fit.

    5

(c) Three no-trump.

    You want the lead to come up to your hand and you hope to make nine tricks in no trumps, so bid three no-trump.

    5

(d) No Bid.

    One does not like passing one club but there is nothing forcing about the opening, using standard methods.

    5

(e) Two spades.

    Forcing to game. It would be quite wrong to burst into Blackwood at this point.

    5

(f) Four hearts = 5 points. One heart = 1 point.

    There should be a good chance to make four hearts and you wish to shut out a possible spade bid from the opponents.

    5

c/f	**180**	

	MAX. AWARD	YOUR SCORE
b/f	**180**	

7(a) Three no-trump.

No reason not to play in no trumps.

5

(b) Three spades = 5 points. Three no-trump = 3 points. Four hearts = 1 point.

Partner is most unlikely to hold four spades as he would bid his major suit rather than no trumps. The object of bidding spades yourself is to confirm that you hold five hearts and can be raised to four hearts on three. To bid four hearts is not really correct with only a five-card suit, but it might be alright as the singleton diamond might be a hazard in no trumps.

5

(c) Three hearts.

Sign off expecting partner to pass. If you thought you could make four hearts you would bid it.

5

(d) Three no-trump.

With a maximum of 31 high card points between you and no long suit a slam is unlikely.

5

(e) Three diamonds = 5 points. Three no-trump = 3 points. Four hearts = 1 point.

The rebid of a new suit is forcing and you wish to convey that you are not entirely suitable for no-trumps and invite preference back to hearts if partner holds three. If partner bids three no-trump, pass.

5

(f) Four hearts.

You expect to make four hearts so bid it. Three hearts would be a sign-off.

5

| **c/f** | **210** | |

	MAX. AWARD	YOUR SCORE
b/f	210	

8(a) Three no-trump = 5 points. Five diamonds = 3 points. Three diamonds = 1 point.

 This is a reasonable gamble of making eight tricks on a heart lead. A pre-emptive five diamonds might produce a good result if partner held a blank hand. If doubled you would go three down, losing 500 (honours do not count in duplicate pairs) and this would be less than the value of a vulnerable game to East-West who might be able to bid and make four hearts or four spades = 620 (120 = 500 bonus for game). A jump overcall of three diamonds is a bit half-hearted but might lead to three no-trump.

| | 5 | |

(b) No Bid.

 You have no other reasonable call.

| | 5 | |

(c) Four spades = 5 points. Three spades = 1 point.

 With no defensive strength but considerable playing strength pre-empt to your limit. You should be able to take eight tricks even if partner has nothing, in which case you have saved a vulnerable game or even slam cheaply.

| | 5 | |

(d) Double = 5 points. Two diamonds = 2 points.

 With four cards in the other major suit (spades) double is superior to a direct overcall in your broken diamond suit. If partner responds two clubs you can still bid two diamonds.

| | 5 | |

| c/f | 230 | |

	MAX. AWARD	YOUR SCORE
b/f	**230**	

8(e) One spade = 5 points. No Bid = 2 points.

    An overcall in a suit is not judged primarily by points but on the number of tricks you can hope to make and the value of the call for lead directing purposes.

    In this case, if your partner is on lead against no trumps you may well be able to set up your suit quickly. If you pass, West may respond two no-trump and be raised to three no-trump, and your partner, knowing nothing of your spades, will lead a club or diamond. A further point is that many players are reluctant to bid up in no-trumps against an intervening bid unless they hold at least two stoppers in the suit. By bidding one spade you may well keep the opponents out of a lay down game.

    5

(f) No Bid = 5 points. Two diamonds = 1 point.

    With 14 high-card points there is no great chance of the opponents making game, especially as you are strong in their suit. To overcall on a broken suit of diamonds may well result in losing 300 or 500 after being doubled, only to find that you have saved nothing. Overcalls should be based on playing strength and on the principle of what you stand to gain against what you stand to lose. Here your hand is of value in defence but not in attack. Some might be tempted to bid one no-trump but the points are too low and the shape is not balanced.

    5

9(a) One no-trump = 5 points. Two clubs = 1 point.

    You hold a good stopper in diamonds, opener's bid. Do not worry about spades as your partner must surely hold strength in this suit on his double of one diamond. A small award is given for two clubs as it is better than passing.

    5

| c/f | **245** | |

	MAX. AWARD	YOUR SCORE
b/f	**245**	

9(b) Double

A penalty double indicating strength in spades. It may be that East is bluffing with his one spade and trying to talk you out of a spade contract. If so your partner can now expose the psychic bid by bidding spades himself.

5

(c) Three no-trump = 5 points. Three clubs = 1 point.

With a diamond stopper and your partner having strength in the major suits, game in no trumps in the best contract. Five clubs will probably fail, particularly with a diamond lead through your K J 10.

5

(d) Two diamonds = 5 points. Two hearts = 1 point.

Bidding opponent's suit is forcing and indicates a good hand, but unsure which is to be the best contract. It does not guarantee first round control in diamonds but merely says "I have a good hand and await your next bid".

5

(e) Four hearts = 5 points.

There should be a fair play for four hearts, so bid it. Three hearts would show a better than minimum hand but would not be forcing.

5

(f) Two hearts = 5 points. Two clubs = 2 points.

With 8 points you are justified in making a free bid and it is better to call the major suit.

5

c/f	**270**	

	MAX. AWARD	YOUR SCORE
b/f	270	

10(a) Two spaces

    This is purely competitive and not strength showing. You are prepared to play in two spades opposite partner's strong no trump and it would be timid to pass and allow opponents to play in two diamonds. If you had a better hand you would make a jump bid in spades or support no trumps.

5

(b) Three hearts.

    Forcing. Partner should raise with three.

5

(c) Three diamonds = 5 points. Three no-trump = 2 points. Double = 2 points.

    You would have bid two clubs Stayman had East passed. Your cue bid in his suit serves a similar purpose, and partner should bid a four card major if he has one. Failing which he bids three no-trump as he must surely hold a diamond stopper. Points are given for double as the contract must surely go down with your marked superiority in high card strength. But the penalty might not necessarily prove adequate.

5

(d) Double = 5 points. Three no-trump = 3 points. Two no-trump = 2 points.

    You should get a good penalty and there is no certainty that you can make game if partner holds a minimum.

5

(e) Three no-trump.

    Partner should have a diamond stopper. He has no high cards in clubs and should not open one no-trump with two unguarded suits. As you can provide six tricks without using up any of his original 15-17 points, he should be able to make three more.

5

(f) Four hearts.

    What you expect to make.

5

| | Total | 300 | |

Rate Your Bidding

Inspired. You only have to match it with your play to be a world beater.

Above average. A reliable bidding partner.

Not so good. You will need to play very well to make some of the curious contracts you may reach.

Max 300	
250-300	
150-250	
150-below	

Part 2
Leading

Leading

11. You are South and the bidding, with East dealer, has been:

S	W	N	E
		–	1 ♠
–	3 ♠	–	4 ♠

What do you lead from

♠ J 10 3   ♡ K J 3   ◇ J 4 3 2   ♣ A J 6

12. You are South, with West dealer. The bidding was:

S	W	N	E
	1 ◇	1 ♡	2 ♠
3 ♡	3 ♠	–	4 ♠
–	4 NT	–	5 ♡
–	6 ♠	Double	–

What do you lead from

♠ 3   ♡ K Q 5 4   ◇ 9 7 4 2   ♣ 10 6 4 3

13. You are South, East dealt and the bidding was:

S	W	N	E
			1 ♡
–	2 ♡	2 ♠	Double
–	3 ♡	–	3 NT
–	4 ♡	–	–

What do you lead from

♠ 5 3 2   ♡ A 7 4   ◇ 6 3 2   ♣ Q 8 6 5

14. You are South and East dealt. The bidding was:

S	W	N	E
			3 ♠
–	4 NT	–	5 ♡
–	7 ♠	–	–

East-West are playing the Culbertson 4-5 No Trump convention so that East's five hearts shows ♡ A. What do you lead from

♠ K 8   ♡ Q 10 9 2   ◊ 10 8 2   ♣ 7 4 3 2

15. You are South with West dealer. The bidding was:

S	W	N	E
	1 ◊	1 ♠	1 NT
–	2 NT	–	3 NT
–	–	Double	–

What do you lead from

♠ 3   ♡ Q 10 9 6 3   ◊ 10 9 6   ♣ 7 6 5 4

16. You are South, East dealt and the bidding was:

S	W	N	E
			1 ♠
2 ♣	Double	Redouble	–
2 ◊	–	–	3 ♠

North's redouble was the Koch-Werner Convention, asking partner to try another suit. What do you lead from

♠ –   ♡ Q 4 3   ◊ A Q 9 2   ♣ K J 9 6 5 2

17. You are South. East dealt and the bidding was:

S	W	N	E
			2 ♣
–	3 ♣	–	3 ♡
–	4 ◊	–	4 NT
–	5 ◊	–	6 NT
–	–	Double	–

What do you lead from

♠ 9 5 4 2   ♡ 6 5 3   ◊ J 10 6   ♣ 9 7 3

18. You are South, East dealt and the bidding was:

S	W	N	E
			1 ♡
Double	2 ♡	–	4 ♡
Double	–	–	–

What do you lead from

♠ K J 10   ♡ 3 2   ◇ A K 10 6   ♣ A K 6 4

19. You are South, East dealt and the bidding was:

S	W	N	E
			3 NT
–	–	–	

What do you lead from

♠ 10 5 2   ♡ A 8 4 3   ◇ A Q 10 8 4   ♣ 4

20. You are South, playing in a pairs tournament. East dealt and the bidding was:

S	W	N	E
			1 NT (16-18 pts.)
–	2 ♣	–	2 ◇
–	3 NT	–	–

West's response was Stayman asking for a four card major suit. What do you lead from

♠ Q J   ♡ Q 5   ◇ 10 7 2   ♣ Q 9 8 5 4 2

21. You are South, East dealt and the bidding was:

S	W	N	E
			1 NT (12-14 pts.)
–	3 NT	–	–

What do you lead from

♠ 6 2   ♡ A 8 6   ◇ K J 10 9 7 6   ♣ 5 3

22. You are South, East dealt and the bidding was:

S	W	N	E
			1 ♦
Double	–	–	–

What do you lead from

♠ K Q 8 6   ♡ A K 2   ♦ 2   ♣ K 9 8 6 4

23. You are South, East dealt and the bidding was:

S	W	N	E
			1 ♦
–	2 ♦	–	3 ♦
–	3 ♡	–	3 NT

What do you lead from

♠ 10 9 2   ♡ K J 6 5 3   ♦ 2   ♣ Q 8 7 4

24. You are South, East dealt and the bidding was:

S	W	N	E
			1 ♠
–	3 ♠	–	6 ♠

What do you lead from

♠ A Q 2   ♡ J 10 2   ♦ J 10 9 3   ♣ K 4 2

25. You are South, East dealt and the bidding was:

S	W	N	E
			1 ♠
–	3 ♠	–	4 ♠

What do you lead from

♠ 9 7 6   ♡ 2   ♦ J 10 9 4 3   ♣ 10 8 6 4

26. You are South, East dealt and the bidding was:

S	W	N	E
			1 ♠
–	3 ♦	–	3 ♠
–	4 NT	–	5 ♣
–	5 ♠	–	–

Four no-trump is Culbertson 4-5 NT Convention and five
clubs shows ♣A. What do you lead from

♠Q 3 2　♡A J 2　◇9 2　♣Q 9 8 7 4

27. You are South, East dealt and the bidding was:

S	W	N	E
			2♠
3◇	3♠	–	4♣
–	4♡	–	4♠
–	5♣	–	6♠

What do you lead from

♠10 9　♡K 8 7 6 4　◇A K J 7 6 2　♣–

28. You are South playing in a Teams match. East dealt at
love all. The bidding was:

S	W	N	E
			1◇
–	1♠	–	1 NT
–	2 NT	–	–

The rebid of one no-trump would show 15-16 points.
What do you lead from

♠9 8 7 4　♡Q J 4　◇J 7　♣A Q 10 6

29. You are South playing Teams of Four. West deals with
East-West vulnerable. The bidding was:

S	W	N	E
	1◇	–	3♣
3♡	4◇	4♡	4 NT
6♡	–	–	6 NT
–	7◇	Double	7 NT
Double	–	–	Redouble

What do you lead from

♠K 10 9　♡K 9 7 6 4 3　◇4　♣10 8 2

30. You are South playing Teams of Four. You dealt at love
    all and the bidding was

S	W	N	E
1 ♡	–	2 ♡	Double
–	4 ♠	–	6 ♣

What do you lead from

♠ Q 6 5   ♡ A 5 4 3 2   ◇ A J 7 2   ♣ 3

Answers

11. ♠ 3.

   With most of the high card strength possessed by your side you should make a passive lead. You should hope for declarer to lose four tricks rather than try to set out to win four tricks. Select a lead that is likely to give no help to declarer.

   It is important to lead a small spade and not an honour. Partner might have singleton king or queen and to lead ♠J might result in your side not making a trump trick at all.

12. A diamond.

   The double of a slam contract by the player not on lead is conventional and called a 'Lightner Double' after its originator, Theodore A. Lightner of New York. The double demands an 'unusual' lead, certainly not a heart which your partner called nor a trump. It almost certainly asks for a diamond in this case, dummy's first bid suit, and it is likely your partner will be void and will ruff.

	MAX. AWARD	YOUR SCORE
11.	5	
12.	5	
c/f	10	

	MAX. AWARD	YOUR SCORE
b/f	**10**	

13. ♡4 = 5 points. ♡A = 4 points.   **5**

Consider the bidding. Your partner has called spades and been doubled. West took out the double and again reverted to hearts after East bid three no-trump. West's hand is not strong but contains ruffing values. He is short in spades; therefore lead a trump to destroy the ruffing power. A low trump is slightly better. Opposing hearts are likely to be 4-4 and partner has a second heart to return if he gets in early. You can then play ace and another trump, reducing declarer and dummy to one each.

14. ♠8.   **5**

This may appear startling but the bidding supplies a clue. The hand on your right showed ♡A and the hand on your left bid seven spades and must have the remaining aces including the ace of trumps. The opening bid indicates a seven-card suit at least, headed by Q J 10 and dummy probably holds A X X. On the lead of a low spade it will be a brave declarer who does not go up with the ace and hope to drop the king.

15. ♠3.   **5**

Your partner's double requests that you lead his suit.

16. ♣2 = 5 points. ♣6 or ♣5 = 3 points.   **5**

Partner's redouble implies a probable void in clubs. You should lead ♣2 as a suit preference signal to indicate a diamond return the lower of the two remaining suits, other than trumps. ♣2 cannot be fourth best as you would not overcall on a four card suit. Therefore, being an abnormally low card it should be read as a signal. Hand from World Pairs Olympiad Cannes, 1962.

c/f	**30**	

	MAX. AWARD	YOUR SCORE
b/f	**30**	

17. A club.
    Partner's double requests the lead of one of
    dummy's suits. It is probably a club, as partner
    had two opportunities of doubling diamonds for
    a lead.

5

18. A trump = 5 points. ◇A or ♣A = 1 point.
    The only way they can make ten tricks is by
    ruffing and dummy is probably short
    somewhere.

5

19. ♡A or ◇A.
    East's opening bid is based on a long solid minor
    suit, in this case clubs. It is essential to hold the
    lead until you see dummy.

5

20. ♠Q = 5 points. ♣5 = 3 points.
    East's denial of a four-card major means he has
    certainly something in clubs. Spades are better
    than hearts and North probably has length
    sitting over dummy.
        In the 1966 World Olympiad Ladies Pairs,
    Mrs Durran and Mrs Juan (now Mrs Priday)
    who won the title for Britain, were one of only
    four pairs to defeat three no-trump on the lead of
    ♠Q.

5

21. ◇K = 5 points. ◇J = 3 points.
    There is a small possibility of felling a singleton
    queen either in dummy or partner's hand. If
    partner does not hold ◇A you are going to lose
    two tricks unless you pin the queen.

5

22. ◇2.
    A trump lead is mandatory when partner passes
    a take-out double for penalties. His diamonds
    must be long and solid and you must try to
    prevent declarer making small trumps with ruffs.
    You are in effect playing the contract yourself in
    diamonds.

5

| **c/f** | **60** | |

	MAX. AWARD	YOUR SCORE
b/f	60	

23. ♡ 5 = 5 points. ♠10 = 2 points.

West does not have a genuine heart suit and his bid is merely a probe for no trumps, indicating a stopper.

| | 5 | |

24. ♠A = 5 points. ◇J = 2 points.

If East has ♠K you always have two trump tricks. But if West has say ♠K 10 X X and East ♠ J 9, X X X he may finesse you for ♠Q. Leading ♠A and following with ♠2 is your best chance of making ♠Q if ♠K turns up in dummy.

| | 5 | |

25. ♡2 = 5 points. Trump = 3 points. ◇J = 2 points.

The opponents have shown no interest in a slam and you have only one point (◇J). There is a reasonable chance that your partner has two aces. If one of these is hearts you should win the first four tricks with two ruffs plus two aces.

A singleton has a better chance of succeeding when your hand is extremely weak, as there is a greater likelihood of partner holding the necessary high cards for you to get a ruff. Conversely, if you hold a fair hand of about 11-12 points a singleton is much less attractive.

| | 5 | |

26. ♡A = 5 points. ♡2 = 1 point.

Opponents appear to be lacking heart control. J. Sharples led ♡A in a Camrose Trophy match against Scotland. Some credit is given to ♡2 but it might lose to a singleton king.

| | 5 | |

| c/f | 80 | |

	MAX. AWARD	YOUR SCORE
b/f	**80**	

27. ◇2.
The best chance is to find partner with ◇Q for a club return. Opponents can hardly have two losing diamonds in each hand. The lead of ◇2, an unnecessarily low card, should be read as a suit preference signal for the return of the lower ranking of the two remaining suits, excluding trumps.

This fine lead was made by Steen Moller of Denmark in the match against Turkey in the 1969 European Championship in Oslo.

	5	

28. ♠9 = 5 points. ♠4 = 4 points. ♡Q = 3 points. ♣6 = 1 point.
This hand occurred in the Ladies European Championship about twenty years ago and the actual lead of ♡Q was disastrous. The problem was put to a panel of experts in the *British Bridge World* magazine and the consensus of opinion was that the passive lead of ♠9 was the best and that ♡Q was likely to cost a trick. One member of the panel called ♡Q "a dreadful lead".

	5	

29. A spade.
If North has a minor suit ace it can hardly run away. In the match between Britain and Belgium in the European Championship in Oslo in 1958 the British defender led a diamond and the contract was made.

	5	

30. ♣3 = 5 points. ◇A = 3 points. ♡A = 2 points.
In the match between Denmark and Switzerland in the 1967 European Championship in Dublin, ♣3 proved the only lead to defeat the contract. The Danish defender unsuccessfully attempted to cash ◇A which appeared to have a better chance than ♡A.

	5	

| **Total** | **100** | |

Rate Your Leading

	Max 100
You should always arrange to be on lead when your side is defending.	75-100
Above average. You will not give many tricks away on the lead.	50- 75
Maybe you are just unlucky. Your best chance is to buy the contracts or hope your partner leads.	50-below

Part 3
Defence

Defence

31. You are West and dealer. North-South are vulnerable. The bidding was:

S	W	N	E
	1 ◊	Double	3 ◊
3 ♠	–	4 ♠	–

                 ♠ A K 8 2
                 ♡ K 8 7
                 ◊ J
                 ♣ A 10 9 7 6

♠ 7 4
♡ A Q 4 2
◊ A K 10 8 5
♣ 8 5

You lead ◊A to which your partner follows with ◊2.

(a)   What do you lead to trick two?
(b)   Why?

32. You are East at love all. South is the dealer. The
    bidding was:

S	W	N	E
1 ◇	–	1 ♡	–
3 NT	–	–	–

         ♠ 8 3 2
         ♡ 10 8 7 2
         ◇ K J 6 4
         ♣ K 2

            ♠ J 10 5
            ♡ A Q 9 3
            ◇ Q 10 2
            ♣ J 10 5

    West leads ♠4 on which you play ♠10 and South wins
    with ♠K. South leads ◇A, West following with ◇3. To
    trick three South leads ◇5, West discards ♣6 and
    dummy plays ◇J, losing to your ◇Q.
     (a) What do you play to trick four?
     (b) Why?

33. You are East with East-West vulnerable. North dealt.
    Bidding was:

S	W	N	E
		1 ◇	Double
4 ♠	–	–	Double

         ♠ 8 5
         ♡ K 6 2
         ◇ A Q J 9 8
         ♣ A Q 6

            ♠ A K 3
            ♡ A 8 7 4 3
            ◇ K 2
            ♣ K J 5

    West leads ♡Q, covered by ♡K and South ruffs your ♡A.
    South next leads ♠Q, West follows with ♠2 and you win
    with ♠K.
     (a) What do you lead to trick three?
     (b) Why?

34. You are West and North – South are vulnerable. South
    dealt. Bidding was:

S	W	N	E
1♣	–	1♦	–
1 NT	–	2 NT	–

North-South are playing a strong no-trump, South's
rebid indicating about 13-14 points

                    ♠ K 7 6
                    ♡ 10 6 3 2
                    ◇ A Q 10 2
                    ♣ Q 4
    ♠ J 10 9 8
    ♡ K 8 4
    ◇ K 8 5
    ♣ A 5 3

You lead ♠J, won in dummy, East playing ♠2. At trick
two ♣Q is led from dummy, East following with ♣2,
South with ♣8 and you with ♣3. Dummy's ♣4 is led,
East following with ♣6, South with ♣9.

    (a)   How do you plan the defence?
    (b)   Why?

35. You are East with both sides vulnerable. North dealt.
    Bidding went:

S	W	N	E
		1♣	–
1♡	–	1♠	–
2 NT	–	3 NT	–

                    ♠ A K J 9
                    ♡ 8 5
                    ◇ 7 5
                    ♣ A Q J 10 6
                            ♠ 7 6 3 2
                            ♡ K Q 7 2
                            ◇ Q J 4
                            ♣ K 3

West leads ◇3 and your ◇J holds the trick, South
playing ◇6.

    (a)   How do you plan the defence?
    (b) Why?

36. You are East, playing match-pointed pairs. It is love all.
    South dealt. Bidding was:

S	W	N	E
1♠	2♡	2♠	4♡
4♠	Double	–	–

            ♠ J 10 7 6
            ♡ 8 5 3
            ◇ J 9
            ♣ K 10 8 4

                       ♠ 3 2
                       ♡ K Q 6
                       ◇ 10 7 6 3
                       ♣ A Q J 7

West leads ♣5, ♣4 is played from dummy and you win
with ♣J, South playing ♣2. You next lead ♡K and West
follows with ♡4, South ♡2.

    (a)   What do you lead to trick three?
    (b) Why?

37. You are East. It is love all and South dealt. Bidding
    went:

S	W	N	E
1♠	–	2♡	–
2♠	–	–	–

            ♠ 5 4
            ♡ A K 8 7 5
            ◇ Q 10 7 6
            ♣ J 2

                       ♠ J 3
                       ♡ Q J 6 2
                       ◇ 8 4
                       ♣ K 10 8 7 6

West leads ◇A to which you play ◇8 and South ◇5. West continues with ◇K to which you follow with ◇4 and South with ◇9. West leads ◇2 which you ruff with ♠3 and South follows with ◇J.

(a)   What do you lead to trick four?
(b)   Why?

38. You are West with North-South vulnerable. North dealt. Bidding was:

S	W	N	E
		1 ◇	–
1 NT	–	3 NT	–

♠ J
♡ A 9
◇ A K Q J 10 7
♣ 9 6 4 2

♠ A 8 6 5
♡ 8 6 5
◇ 8 3 2
♣ K Q 3

You lead ♠5 covered by ♠J, ♠K and ♠9. East returns ♠2, South following with ♠10.

(a)   How do you plan the defence?
(b)   Why?

39. You are East with North-South vulnerable. North dealt. Bidding was:

S	W	N	E
		1 ♣	1 ♠
1 NT	–	3NT	–

♠ Q 2
♡ 7 3
◇ A Q 8
♣ A K Q J 8 2

♠ A J 10 9 4
♡ A 6 2
◇ 10 9
♣ 9 7 3

West leads ♠7 and ♠2 is played from dummy.

    (a)   How do you plan the defence?
    (b)   Why?

40. You are West at game all. Dealer South. Bidding went:

S	W	N	E
1 ♠	–	3 ♦	–
3 ♠	–	4 ♠	–
4 NT	–	5 ♡	Double
–	–	6 ♦	–
6 ♠	–	–	–

               ♠ A 2
               ♡ 2
               ♦ A K J 10 7 6 4
               ♣ 7 5 3

♠ J 5 3
♡ A K 4 3
♦ 9 2
♣ 10 8 4 2

You lead ♡A on which East plays ♡Q.

    (a)   What do you lead to trick two?
    (b)   Why?

41. You are West, the dealer at love all. Bidding was:

S	W	N	E
	1 ♣	2 ♡	4 ♣
4 ♦	4 ♠	–	–
5 ♦	–	–	–

               ♠ 6 5
               ♡ A J 10 9 7 3 2
               ♦ A 2
               ♣ Q 6

♠ A K Q 2
♡ 5 4
♦ Q
♣ K 9 8 7 5 4

You lead ♠A, followed by ♠Q. East followed with ♠4 and ♠3.

   (a)   What do you lead to trick three?

   (b)   Why?

42. You are East at love all. South dealt. Bidding went:

S	W	N	E
1 ♦	–	1 ♠	–
3 ♦	–	–	–

                    ♠ K 10 8 5 3
                    ♡ Q 4
                    ♦ 5 3
                    ♣ 10 8 3 2

                                ♠ Q 9 6
                                ♡ K 10 8 6
                                ♦ 4 2
                                ♣ Q J 9 5

West leads ♣A (Ace from Ace-King) and ♣2 is played from the table.

   (a)   What do you play to the first trick?

   (b)   How do you plan the defence.

43. You are West with North-South vulnerable. South dealt. Bidding was:

S	W	N	E
1 ♡	Double	Redouble	–
–	2 ♦	3 ♡	–
4 ♡	–	–	–

                    ♠ A J 3
                    ♡ K J 7 5
                    ♦ 9 3
                    ♣ Q J 9 4

♠ K 10 9
♡ A 2
♦ Q J 10 7 4
♣ K 8 3

You lead ◇Q to which East follows with ◇2 and South wins with ◇A. South leads ♡6 to trick two.

   (a)   What do you play to trick two?
   (b)   How do you plan the defence?

44. You are West with East-West vulnerable. North dealt. Bidding went:

S	W	N	E
		1♣	1◇
1♠	4◇	4♠	–

                   ♠ Q J 4 2
                   ♡ K Q 3 2
                   ◇ –
                   ♣ K Q J 10 9

♠ K 3
♡ 10 8
◇ A 10 7 6 5 4
♣ 4 3 2

You lead ◇A ruffed in dummy, East playing ◇Q and South ◇K. At trick two ♠Q is played from dummy, East playing ♠6, South ♠5 and you win with ♠K.

   (a)   What do you lead to trick three?
   (b)   Why?

45. You are West at love all. South dealt. Bidding went:

S	W	N	E
1♣	–	1◇	–
1♡	–	3♣	–
3NT	–	–	–

                   ♠ K 7
                   ♡ 10
                   ◇ Q J 7 3 2
                   ♣ Q 8 7 4 2

♠ Q 8 3
♡ 9 7 4 3 2
◇ K 10 8 4
♣ 5

You decide to lead ♠3 to which ♠7 is played from dummy. East plays ♠J and South ♠2. East cashes ♠A covered by ♠4, ♠8 and ♠K. To trick three East returns ♠5, South plays ♠10 and you win with ♠Q.

    (a)   What do you lead to trick four?
    (b)   Why?

46. You are West at game all. South dealt. Bidding was:

S	W	N	E
1 ♠	–	1 NT	–
3 ♣	–	3 NT	–
4 ♠	–	5 ♣	–

              ♠ 10
              ♡ J 10 9 7
              ◇ K Q 2
              ♣ Q 9 7 4 2

♠ Q 9 5 4 2
♡ A 6 3
◇ A J 5
♣ 6 3

You lead ♡A on which East plays ♡2 and South ♡K.

    (a)   What should you lead to trick two?
    (b)   Why?

47. You are East with East-West vulnerable. North dealt. Bidding was:

S	W	N	E
		1 ◇	2 ♣
2 ♡	–	4 ♡	–

              ♠ A Q J
              ♡ 9 7 6 4
              ◇ A K Q 5
              ♣ 4 3

                          ♠ 8 5 3
                          ♡ A
                          ◇ 8 6 3
                          ♣ A K J 10 8 5

West leads ♣6 which you win with ♣K, South playing ♣9. You next play ♣A, South following with ♣Q and West ♣7. You are playing M U D (middle-up-down) so West still holds ♣2.

  (a) What do you lead to trick three?

  (b) Why?

48. You are East at game all. North dealt. Bidding was:

S	W	N	E
		1 ◇	1 ♠
2 NT	–	3 NT	–
	–		

         ♠ J
         ♡ A K J
         ◇ Q J 9 8 5 3
         ♣ K 9 4

                  ♠ A Q 10 4 3 2
                  ♡ 8 6 3
                  ◇ A 4
                  ♣ 8 7

West leads ♠6.

  (a) What do you play to the first trick?

  (b) Why?

49. You are East at game all. West dealt. Bidding was:

S	W	N	E
	–	1 ♠	–
2 ♡	–	2 ♠	–
3 ◇	Double	4 ♡	–
4 NT	–	5 ◇	–
6 ♡	–	–	–

         ♠ K 10 9 8 6 5
         ♡ J 9
         ◇ 9
         ♣ A K Q J

                  ♠ J 7 2
                  ♡ K 8 5 3
                  ◇ 7
                  ♣ 10 9 7 4 2

West leads ◊K, taken by South with ◊A. South leads
♡2, West playing ♡6, dummy ♡J and you win with ♡K.

    (a)   What do you lead to trick three?
    (b)   Why?

50. You are East with North-South vulnerable. South dealt.
    Bidding went:

S	W	N	E
1♣	–	2◊	–
2♡	–	3♡	–
4♡	–	4♠	–
4 NT	–	5♡	–
5 NT	–	6♠	–
7♡	–	–	–

    ♠ A K 3
    ♡ A K J 5
    ◊ K 8 5 4 3
    ♣ 2

                  ♠ J 7 2
                  ♡ 6 4 3
                  ◊ J 10 7 6 2
                  ♣ Q 4

West leads ♡10, taken with ♡J. Declarer leads ♣2 to his
♣A, West following with ♣5. South next leads ♣6, ruffed
in dummy with ♡5, West following with ♣3. He next
plays ◊3 from the table to his ◊Q, West following with
◊9. South next leads ♣8, covered by West with ♣9 and
ruffed in dummy with ♡K.

    (a)   What should East discard?
    (b)   Why?

51. You are East, the dealer, at game all. Bidding was:

S	W	N	E
			1 NT (15-17)
2 ♠	3 ♣	4 ♠	–
–	5 ♣	5 ◇	–
5 ♠	–	–	–

♠ 10 4 3
♡ 9 4
◇ A K Q 10 9 6 3
♣ 5

♠ Q 5 2
♡ A 8 5
◇ J 8 5 2
♣ A K J

West leads ◇7, taken in dummy with ◇Q. Declarer leads ♠3 from the table, covered by ♠2, ♠A and ♠J. South next plays ♣2, taken by your ♣J.

(a) What do you lead to trick four?
(b) Why?

52. You are West and North-South are vulnerable. South dealt and the bidding was:

S	W	N	E
2 ♠	–	2 NT	3 ◇
4 ♠	–	–	–

♠ 10 3
♡ J 10 8 4
◇ K 5 3
♣ Q 7 6 3

♠ A 9 4
♡ 6 2
◇ 10 9 2
♣ K 10 8 5 2

You lead ◇10 which wins and continue with ◇9, ruffed by South. South leads ♠K to which you play ♠4 and East

♠2. South continues with ♠Q which you take with ♠A, East discarding a diamond.

    (a)   What do you lead to trick five?

    (b)   Why?

53. You are East at love all. North dealt and bidding went:

S	W	N	E
		1 NT	–
4 ♠	–	–	–

        ♠ J 7 2
        ♡ Q 8 6 5
        ◊ A Q J
        ♣ K 5 2

                ♠ A 8 6
                ♡ A
                ◊ 9 8 5 3 2
                ♣ A Q 7 4

West leads ♡J to your ♡A.

    (a)   What do you lead to trick two?

    (b)   Why?

54. You are East, the dealer, with North-South vulnerable.
    Bidding went:

S	W	N	E
			2 ♠ (weak –
–	–	3 ◇	– 5-9 points)
3 NT	–	–	–

                    ♠ K 10
                    ♡ 4 2
                    ◇ K Q 10 8 5
                    ♣ A 7 5 2

                              ♠ A 8 7 6 5 2
                              ♡ J 7 6 3
                              ◇ J 4
                              ♣ 8

West leads ♠9 and ♠K is played from dummy.

   (a)   How do you plan the defence?
   (b)   Why?

55. You are East with North-South vulnerable. South dealt.
    Bidding was:

S	W	N	E
1 ♠	2 ♡	3 ◇	3 ♡
3 ♠	–	4 ♠	–

                    ♠ A 9 4
                    ♡ 4
                    ◇ K Q 8 7 5
                    ♣ Q J 7 3

                              ♠ 7 6 5
                              ♡ K 6 3
                              ◇ 4 2
                              ♣ A 9 6 5 4

West leads ♣2 and ♣3 is played from dummy.

   (a)   How do you plan the defence?
   (b)   Why?

56. You are East with North-South vulnerable. North dealt.
   Bidding was:

S	W	N	E
		1 ♡	–
2 ♣	–	2 ◇	–
2 NT	–	3 NT	Double

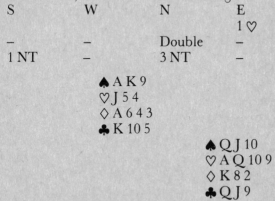

```
        ♠ Q 6
        ♡ A J 9 7
        ◇ A K 8 4
        ♣ 9 4 3
                    ♠ 4 2
                    ♡ K Q 10 6 4
                    ◇ Q 6 5 2
                    ♣ A 2
```

In answer to your lead-directing double West starts with
♡8 and ♡9 is played from the table.

   (a) What do you play to the first trick?
   (b) Why?

57. You are East, dealer at love all. Bidding went:

S	W	N	E
			1 ♡
–	–	Double	–
1 NT	–	3 NT	–

```
        ♠ A K 9
        ♡ J 5 4
        ◇ A 6 4 3
        ♣ K 10 5
                    ♠ Q J 10
                    ♡ A Q 10 9
                    ◇ K 8 2
                    ♣ Q J 9
```

West leads ♡8, dummy plays ♡4 and your ♡9 is taken
with South's ♡K. South leads ◇Q to which West follows
with ◇7 and you win with ◇K.

   (a) How do you plan the defence?
   (b) Why?

58. You are West and East-West are vulnerable. South dealt. Bidding:

S	W	N	E
4♡	–	–	–

♠ J 6 5 4
♡ 2
◇ A J 6 5
♣ K 10 6 3

♠ A K Q 2
♡ A 3
◇ 10 9 8 7
♣ Q J 4

You lead ♠A to which dummy plays ♠4, East ♠3 and South ♠9. You continue with ♠Q to which dummy plays ♠5. East ♠7 and South ♠10.

(a) What do you lead to trick three?
(b) Why?

59. You are West at love all. South dealt. Bidding went:

S	W	N	E
1◇	1♠	2◇	–
2♡	–	4♡	–

♠ 10 8 3 2
♡ 9 8 7 6
◇ A J 7
♣ K Q

♠ K Q J 9 4
♡ K 5 4 2
◇ 6 2
♣ 8 6

You lead ♠K which East overtakes with ♠A and returns ♠7, South following with ♠5 and ♠6.

(a) What do you lead next?
(b) Why?

60. You are East, the dealer, with East-West vulnerable.
   Bidding:

S	W	N	E
			1 NT (16-18 pts.)
2 ♠	–	–	–

   ♠ Q 8
   ♡ Q J 9 6 2
   ◇ K 4 3
   ♣ Q 9 5

   ♠ A 6 5
   ♡ A K 3
   ◇ Q J 10
   ♣ K J 8 3

West leads ♣A to which you follow with ♣8. West
continues with ♣2 and you win with ♣J.

   (a)   How do you plan the defence?
   (b)   Why?

Answers

	MAX. AWARD	YOUR SCORE

31 (a) ♡Q

    (b) The only real chance of defeating the contract is that East has a club trick and that you can establish two heart tricks. If declarer has ♡J you need to find partner with ♡ 10 9 X. After ♡Q is taken by ♡K you hope that East, when in with a club, can lead ♡10 through South's J X.

      South held ♠ Q J 10 9 6 ♡ J 5 3 ◇ 6 4 ♣ K 3 2.

(max. award for this section: 5, 5)

32 (a) ♡A.

    (b) With ♠ 3 2 visible in dummy, West has led from a four card suit. When he discards on the second diamond his distribution must be 4-4-1-4; otherwise he would have a five card suit to lead. Therefore South must hold a singleton heart, and in case this is the king East must lead ♡A. Assuming ♡K falls from South, a low heart to West's ♡J will enable him to return a low heart while you hold ♡Q 9 over ♡10 8. American, Walter Malowan, found this defence.

      South held ♠ A K 9 ♡ K ◇ A 9 8 7 5 ♣ A Q 4 3.

(max. award for this section: 5, 5)

33 (a) ♣5 = 5 points. ♣K or ♣J = 2 points.

    (b) Assuming ◇K takes a trick you can see three tricks and the fourth can only come from clubs. It is no use waiting for clubs to be led to you as the diamonds will be set up and South's losing clubs discarded. You must try and set up a club while you hold two further entries (♠A and ◇K)

c/f   25

	MAX. AWARD	YOUR SCORE
b/f	25	

and hope partner holds ♣10. It is better to lead
♣5 as declarer might hold ♣ 10 8 X and
misguess.

Südafrica

South actually held ♠ Q J 10 9 6 4 2   ♡ –
◇ 107 5   ♣ 9 8 4.

| | 5 | |

34 (a) Win with ♣A and switch to ♡8.

| | 5 | |

(b) South appears to hold five clubs, probably ♣
K J 10 9 8, as East did not peter to indicate a
doubleton. East's holding is probably ♣ 7 6 2.
Nine tricks will be made unless you can make
four tricks in hearts. This will be possible if
South holds, for example, ♡ Q 9 and East
♡ A J 7 5.

South held ♠ A Q 5   ♡ Q 9   ◇ J 9 6
♣ K J 10 9 6.

| | 5 | |

35 (a) Play ◇Q. If it holds switch to ♡2.

| | 5 | |

(b) West appears to have led from a five-card
suit headed by the king and South cannot afford
to take the return of ◇Q. As dummy holds 15
points and you have 11 and partner 3, the
remaining 11 points must be with South. In
other words, West cannot have an entry and it is
pointless continuing with diamonds.

You must hope to set up two tricks in hearts
whilst controlling the clubs with ♣K. The lead of
a low heart will almost certainly succeed if
partner holds ♡ 10 X or ♡ 10 X X as South,
with ♡ A J 9 X will cover with ♡9, the correct
percentage play. A heart return will enable you
to force out ♡A with ♡Q and the defence will
make two diamonds, two hearts and one club.
To lead a heart honour is inferior as you will not
be able to take two heart tricks. Moreover, if
West should happen to hold ♡J, South having
stretched a bit with 10 points, the suit will be
blocked if he has J X.

| | 5 | |
| **c/f** | 50 | |

	MAX. AWARD	YOUR SCORE
b/f	**50**	

36 (a) ♣7.

(b) West's lead is either a singleton, or a doubleton from ♣ 5 3. Had it been a doubleton West would overtake ♡K with ♡A and return ♣3. When he plays low on ♡K, East should return ♣7 for West to ruff and retain ♣ A Q over dummy's ♣ K 10.

As this is a match point tournament it is essential to defeat the contract by three tricks for a penalty of 500, a better score than 420 for making a non-vulnerable game (120 + 300).

South held ♠ K Q 9 8 5   ♡2   ◇ A K 4 ♣ 9 6 3 2.

(Max award column: 5, 5)

37 (a) ♣K.

(b) You intend to continue with a low club to partner's ♣A. Partner should lead a fourth diamond for you to ruff with ♠J, hoping to promote a trump if partner holds 10 X X. If you return a low club, South can discard his second club on your ♠J when you ruff. Partner should hold ♣A on his return of ◇2, his lowest diamond and the prompt cashing of ♣K and ♣A is similar to the situation with cross trumping, when it is important to cash side winners first.

South held ♠ A K Q 8 7 6   ♡ 10 9 ◇ J 9 5   ♣ Q 3.

(Max award column: 5, 5)

38 (a) Win with ♠A and switch to ♣3 = 5 points.
Switch to ♣K = 2 points.

(b) On the play to the first two tricks East is marked with five spades headed by the king, and South with ♠ Q 10 9. South therefore has eight top tricks and a ninth if he holds ♣A. West must take the second spade and switch to ♣3. East may hold ♣ A X in which case it would cost to lead ♣ K or ♣ Q.

South held ♠ Q 10 9   ♡ K Q J   ◇ 9 5 4 ♣ 10 8 7 5.

(Max award column: 5, 5)

| **c/f** | **80** | |

	MAX. AWARD	YOUR SCORE
b/f	**80**	

39 (a) Play ♠A and switch to ♡2 = 5 points.
Switch to ♡A = 1 point.

5

(b) Normally one would play ♠9 with a view to
setting up spades having ♡A as entry. But
looking at dummy it is clear that this plan will
not work as South, if allowed to win the first trick
with ♠K, will cash six clubs and probably three
diamonds. If he has not ◇K himself the finesse
will be right if it is needed, giving nine tricks. (six
clubs, one spade and two diamonds).

The only chance to beat the contract is in
hearts, hoping partner holds something like ♡ K
J 9 X, leaving South ♡ Q 10 8 X. It is important
to lead ♡2. If ♡A is led it will not be possible to
lead through South twice.

South held ♠ K 8 3   ♡ Q 10 8 4
◇ K J 5   ♣ 10 6 4.

5

40 (a) A diamond.

5

(b) South is only likely to make the contract if
he can make dummy's diamonds. The danger is
that he holds ◇Q singleton, in which case it is
essential to lead the suit at once to kill dummy.

5

41 (a) ♠K.

5

(b) South is probably void in clubs as partner is
likely to have five. Leading ♠K will force dummy
to ruff and protect your partner if he has
◇ J X X.

5

42 (a) ♣Q.

5

(b) This implies possession of ♣J and partner
should lead a low club at trick two. It will then
be possible to lead a trump from the East hand
and prevent a heart ruff in dummy.

5

| **c/f** | **120** | |

	MAX. AWARD	YOUR SCORE
b/f	**120**	
	5	

43 (a) ♡A.

(b) Switch to ♠K. Even if partner holds ♡Q South is likely to guess right on the bidding if you duck ♡6. With only one trump trick you must hope for three tricks in the black suits. East can hardly hold ♣A but might have ♠Q. By leading ♠K partner will get in with either the second or third lead of the suit and can return a club to your king. If you lead ♠10 instead of ♠K declarer will cover with ♠J, losing to ♠Q and win the return with ♠A. After drawing trumps and eliminating diamonds you will be put in with ♠9 and forced to lead from ♣K or concede a ruff and discard.

If East returns a club when in with ♠Q, South will be able to discard a spade on ♣Q.

If you were to duck ♡6, South could get home by going up with ♡K and switching to ace and another club, for you would have to ruff the fourth round with ♡A.

This hand occurred in the 1966 Easter International Tournament in London and South held: ♠8742   ♡Q10986   ◊AK   ♣A5.

		5	

44 (a) ♡8.

| | | 5 | |

(b) The only chance of defeating the contract is to make two tricks in hearts and one in clubs. Partner needs to hold ♣A and ♡AJX. His play of ◊Q on the first round, whilst indicating ◊J, might also be construed as a request for a lead of the higher ranking suit (hearts). But in any case a heart lead is essential to set up tricks before the clubs are established.

It is important to lead ♡8 and not ♡10 so that partner, having taken ♡Q with ♡A, can return the suit. If you lead ♡10, covered by ♡Q and ♡A, partner cannot safely return the suit for fear of giving declarer a trick with ♡9.

		5	
c/f	**140**	

	MAX. AWARD	YOUR SCORE
b/f	**140**	

45 (a) Low diamond.   5

(b) On the bidding South probably holds four clubs and four hearts. He is also likely to hold four spades. With a holding of ♠ 10 4 2 opposite ♠ K 7, the king would be played at trick one, as representing the best chance of winning a trick. If South holds ♠ 10 4 2 and East ♠ A J 9 6 5 the correct return would be ♠ 6, original fourth highest.

It is essential for the defence to establish a diamond trick before ♡A is knocked out. South is marked with a singleton diamond.

This hand from a duplicate pairs tournament featured in the *Daily Telegraph Book of Bridge*.

South held ♠ 10 9 4 2   ♡ K Q J 6   ◇ A ♣ A K 9 6.   5

46 (a) ♠Q.   5

(b) It is tempting to try and cash ◇A but there is no hurry as declarer will find it hard to get to dummy. If his clubs are headed by A K and he holds ♠A there is little chance. The best hope is that partner is void in spades or has a possible trump trick. A void is less likely but he may well have a singleton and possibly ♣ K X. In this case you can succeed by leading ♠Q (you cannot afford to risk ♠10 winning). If South attempts to ruff a spade, East will over-ruff. If South leads a diamond, win with ◇A and play a second spade.   5

47 (a) A third club.   5

(b) You have one more sure winner – ♡A. There are no tricks to be won in spades or diamonds. If South lacks ♠K (unlikely) the finesse is right. The only chance is to promote a trump trick for your partner. First you must draw out his last club. This gives a ruff and discard, but no discard can possibly help South. When in with

c/f	**165**	

	MAX. AWARD	YOUR SCORE
b/f	**165**	

♡A play a fourth club and this will promote a trump trick for your partner if he started with either ♡ Q X or ♡ J X X.

| | **5** | |

48 (a) ♠4.

(b) South is marked with ♠ K 9 8 7 and you must hope partner holds ♠5 and an early entry such as ◇K. If you play ♠Q South will duck and it will not be possible for you to establish and enjoy your suit. If you play ♠4 and partner wins the first diamond lead with ◇K and is able to return a spade, you can clear your suit whilst holding ◇A as an entry.

This hand featured in the 1951 Australian World Olympic and South held ♠ K 9 8 7 ♡ Q 10 4   ◇ 10 7 2   ♣ A Q 5.

| | **5** | |
| | **5** | |

49 (a) A club.

(b) Partner must be assumed to hold ♡10 to make declarer's play reasonable and you hope to make a second trump trick. A club return breaks the communications needed to enable declarer to shorten his trumps and pick up your trumps with progressive spade leads.

This hand occurred in the Denmark-Hungary match in the 1969 European Championship in Oslo and was reported by Steen Moller in the official bulletin.

South held ♠ A Q   ♡ A Q 7 4 2   ◇ A 10 8 6 ♣ 8 6

| | **5** | |
| | **5** | |

50 (a) A heart i.e. under-ruff.

(b) In order to enable you to retain three spades including ♠J so that partner can release his spades and protect clubs. In a 1966 Gold Cup match East discarded a low spade and West was later squeezed in the black suits.

| | **5** | |
| | **5** | |

| **c/f** | **200** | |

	MAX. AWARD	YOUR SCORE
b/f	**200**	

51 (a) ♣A or ♣K.   **5**
(b) On the bidding East will certainly be played for ♠Q and West's ♠J will be assumed to be a singleton. South is known to hold a singleton diamond and probably a doubleton club as West is likely to hold a seven card suit, having bid up to five clubs on a queen high suit. South needs two entries to dummy, one to finesse trumps and another to play towards ♡K.
    In the 1969 European Championship in Oslo East led ♡A and the contract was made.
    South held ♠A K 9 8 7 6   ♡K 10 3 2
◇ 4   ♣6 2.   **5**

52 (a) Trump.   **5**
(b) You must retain your third diamond as an exit card. If you return a diamond, declarer will ruff, draw your last trump and play ace and another club. In with ♣K you will either have to give dummy a trick with ♣Q or give South a free finesse in hearts.
    South held ♠ K Q J 8 7 6 5   ♡A K 3
◇ 7   ♣A 4.   **5**

53 (a) ♣Q.   **5**
(b) There is no chance of your partner getting in to play clubs. The best chance is to find him with ♣J. You plan to win the first round of trumps and return a low club and get a heart ruff.
    This problem first appeared in a 1957 British Bridge World Par Contest and South held
♠K Q 10 9 5 3 ♡K 4 ◇ K 10 4 ♣10 9.   **5**

54 (a) Take with ♠A and switch to ♡J.   **5**
(b) The best chance is to hope partner holds ♡A Q 10 X. Declarer probably holds ◇A.
    If you ducked the first round, intending to win a continuation of ♠10 with ♠A and then switch

| **c/f** | **235** | |

	MAX. AWARD	YOUR SCORE
b/f	**235**	

to hearts – score a total of 5 points out of 10 for the two-part question. The danger is that South may collect nine tricks with diamonds and clubs if allowed to take the first trick.   **5**

55 (a) Win with ♣A and returns ♣9.   **5**
(b) Partner's lead looks like a singleton. Return of ♣9 is a simple suit preference signal indicating that you want a return in the higher ranking suit (hearts). You hope partner holds ♡A, having called the suit, and that he will underlead his ace to give you the lead with ♡K.
    South held ♠KQJ108 ♡952 ♢A6 ♣K108.   **5**

56 (a) ♡6.   **5**
(b) If you play ♡10 you cannot make any immediate headway with your hearts. You must hope that your partner can get in and lead a second heart before your entry (♣A) has been forced out.   **5**

57 (a) Cash only two more hearts and switch to ♠Q.   **5**
(b) If you cash the last heart giving your side four tricks you will later be squeezed in clubs and spades when South cashes his diamonds.
    You must hope South has only three clubs and three spades. You can now afford to discard a heart on the last diamond and make a spade and a club.   **5**

58 (a) ♠K.   **5**
(b) South will ruff, but when you regain the lead with ♡A you can lead a fourth spade for East to ruff, forcing South to over-ruff. This will remove the menace of ♠J in dummy and save you from being squeezed in clubs and spades.

c/f	**280**	

	MAX. AWARD	YOUR SCORE
b/f	280	

59 (a) Lead a low spade for East to ruff and force South to over-ruff.

5

(b) South is marked with a four card heart suit and now has three. Plan to hold up ♡K to third round at which point South has no trumps and dummy one. Force dummy's last trump with a high spade.

South held ♠ 6 5   ♡ A Q J 10   ◇ K Q 10 9 5 ♣ A J.

5

60 (a) Return ♣3 for West to ruff.

5

(b) West should play back a trump. A second round of trumps will remove both of dummy's and the defence should make one top trump, one ruff and three clubs and one heart. If you cash ♣K and play a fourth, dummy over-ruffs your partner.

South held ♠ K J 10 9 4 3   ♡ 5   ◇ A 5 ♣ 10 7 6 4.

5

| Total | 300 | |

Rate Your Defence

	Max 300
Very good indeed. Opponents will realise they cannot afford to overbid against you.	250-300
Above average. Clearly you are a competent defender.	150-250
Much room for improvement. Maybe you are better as declarer?	150-below

Part 4
Declarer Play

Declarer Play

61. You are South, declarer in four spades. No opposition bidding.

    N

             ♠ J 8 7 2
             ♡ A 6 5
             ◇ 6
             ♣ Q J 10 6 5

    S

             ♠ K Q 10 9 6
             ♡ K 7 4
             ◇ K 8 7
             ♣ K 4

West leads ♡Q.   Plan the play.

62. You are South, declarer in three no-trump. No opposition bidding.

    N

             ♠ A 6 4
             ♡ K 8 2
             ◇ A 10 4 2
             ♣ 7 4 3

    S

             ♠ K 9 7
             ♡ A Q 6
             ◇ J 7 5 3
             ♣ A K 6

West leads ♡3.   Plan the play.

63. You are South, declarer in seven diamonds. No opposition bidding.

    N   ♠ J 9
                 ♡ A 9 7 3
                 ◊ K Q J
                 ♣ A J 6 3

    S   ♠ A K Q 6 3
                 ♡ Q 8
                 ◊ A 10 8 5 3
                 ♣ 9

    West leads ♣K.   Plan the play.

64. You are South in an optimistic contract of six hearts, with no opposition bidding.

    N   ♠ A J 6 5 4
                 ♡ K J 9
                 ◊ Q 6 5
                 ♣ A 4

    S   ♠ 7 2
                 ♡ A Q 10 8 7
                 ◊ A K 10 2
                 ♣ 9 2

    West leads ♣Q.   Plan the play.

65. You are South, declarer in four spades (opening bid).

    N   ♠ –
                 ♡ Q 7 4 2
                 ◊ K Q 6 5 2
                 ♣ J 9 5 4

    S   ♠ K 10 9 8 7 5 4 3 2
                 ♡ 3
                 ◊ A 7 3
                 ♣ –

    West leads ♣K.   Plan the play.

66. You are South, declarer in three no-trump with no
    opposition bidding.

    N   ♠ 5 2
                ♡ A 8 4 3
                ◊ 7 6 2
                ♣ A 8 7 3

    S   ♠ A 7 6
                ♡ K 5 2
                ◊ A K 5 4 3
                ♣ K 6

    West leads ♠K.

    (a) Plan the play.
    (b) Would it make any difference if dummy held
        ♠ 5 3 2   ♡ A 8 4   ◊ 7 6 2   ♣ A 8 7 3?

67. You are South in four spades with no opposition
    bidding.

    N   ♠ 7 4 3
                ♡ J 8 6 3
                ◊ Q J
                ♣ 10 7 5 3

    S   ♠ Q J 10 6 5 2
                ♡ A
                ◊ A 3 2
                ♣ A K Q

    West leads ♡K.   Plan the play.

68. You are South in an optimistic contract of six hearts,
    West having overcalled your opening bid of one heart
    with one spade.

    N   ♠ 7 6 3 2
                ♡ A Q 8 6
                ◊ 8 5
                ♣ A 9 6

    S   ♠ A 10 5
                ♡ K J 10 9 5
                ◊ A K 6
                ♣ K 7

    West leads ◊Q.   Trumps split 2-2. Plan the play.

69. You are South in three no-trump with no opposition
    bidding.

    N   ♠ Q J 4 2
                        ♡ A K 6
                        ◇ K J 7 6 2
                        ♣ 5

    S   ♠ K 10 5
                        ♡ Q 7 3 2
                        ◇ Q 5 3
                        ♣ A K 10

West leads ♣6 and East plays ♣J.   Plan the play.

70. You are South, declarer in three no-trump after the
    bidding had gone:

S	W	N	E
		1 ◇	1 ♠
3 NT	–	–	–

    N   ♠ 6 5
                        ♡ A 10 7
                        ◇ K 10 8 7 6 5 3
                        ♣ A

    S   ♠ A 10 2
                        ♡ K 9 3
                        ◇ A 2
                        ♣ K 8 6 5 3

West leads ♠4.   Plan the play.

71. You are South, declarer in six spades. East-West vulnerable. The bidding was:

S	W	N	E
2♠	–	3♠	–
4◇	–	5◇	–
5♡	–	6♠	–

N
    ♠ 6 3 2
    ♡ K J 8
    ◇ A 7 4 2
    ♣ K J 5

S
    ♠ A K Q J 9 8 4
    ♡ –
    ◇ K Q 9 8 6
    ♣ 4

West leads ♡4 and East covers ♡J with ♡Q. Trumps are 2-1. Plan the play.

72. You are South, declarer in three no-trump with no opposition bidding.

N
    ♠ 10 8 3
    ♡ 10 6 4
    ◇ Q J 8 6
    ♣ A 7 5

S
    ♠ A 9 7
    ♡ A Q 2
    ◇ A K 2
    ♣ K J 6 2

West leads ♠5 to which East follows with ♠Q. Plan the play.

73. You are South, declarer in four hearts after this
    bidding:

S	W	N	E
1 ♡	Double	2 NT	–
4 ♡	–	–	–

    North's two no-trump should be equivalent to a raise from
    one heart to three hearts had West not doubled.

    N   ♠ 7 3 2
                  ♡ Q 10 3 2
                  ◇ K 4 2
                  ♣ A Q 3

    S   ♠ K 4
                  ♡ A K J 8 5
                  ◇ A 6 5
                  ♣ J 7 4

    West leads ◇Q.   Trumps divide 2-2.   Plan the play.

74. You are South, declarer in six hearts with no opposition
    bidding.

    N   ♠ K 8 6
                  ♡ A 9 4
                  ◇ K 8 5 3
                  ♣ A 7 3

    S   ♠ A J
                  ♡ K Q J 8 7 5
                  ◇ –
                  ♣ K 8 6 5 4

    West leads ◇Q.   Plan the play.

75. You are South, declarer in three no-trump after this
    bidding.

S	W	N	E
			1 ♡
Double	–	2 ◊	–
2 NT	–	3 NT	–

    N   ♠ 8 5
              ♡ 10 7 4 2
              ◊ A 9 6 3
              ♣ K 5 4

    S   ♠ Q J 7 6 3
              ♡ A Q 5
              ◊ K J 7
              ♣ A Q

    West leads ♣2.   Plan the play.

76. You are South, declarer in three no-trump after this
    bidding. East dealer with North-South vulnerable.

S	W	N	E
			–
1 ◊	–	1 ♠	Double
Redouble	2 ♡	–	–
2 NT	–	3 NT	–

    N   ♠ A K 8 6 4
              ♡ 9 3
              ◊ J 6 5
              ♣ K Q 8

    S   ♠ J 10
              ♡ A Q
              ◊ A K 10 9 8
              ♣ J 4 3 2

    West leads ♡6.   Plan the play.

77. You are South, declarer in four spades after this bidding at love all.

S	W	N	E
		1 ◇	1 ♡
1 ♠	2 ♡	4 ♠	−

N
♠ K 8 6 2
♡ A 2
◇ A Q J 2
♣ K J 5

S
♠ Q J 10 9 5
♡ 9 6
◇ 8 6 3
♣ A 6 2

West leads ♡Q.   Trumps split 2-2.   Plan the play.

78. You are South, declarer in six spades, with no opposition bidding.

N
♠ J 7 5 2
♡ A Q 5
◇ Q 3
♣ K Q 10 4

S
♠ A K 6 4 3
♡ K 6
◇ A 6 5
♣ A J 5

West leads ◇J. You play ◇Q from dummy and take East's ◇K with ◇A. You next lead ♠ A K and East discards a diamond on the second round. Plan the play.

79. You are South, declarer in four spades after this
    bidding:

S	W	N	E
	1 ◇	–	2 ◇
4 ♠	–	–	–

N
   ♠ 6 5 3
   ♡ 9 8 6
   ◇ A 3 2
   ♣ Q J 8 7

S
   ♠ A K J 10 9 7 4
   ♡ A K 4
   ◇ 6
   ♣ 6 3

West leads ♣A and switches to ◇K. Plan the play.

80. You are South, declarer in six hearts with no opposition
    bidding.

N
   ♠ A K 5
   ♡ 6 5 3
   ◇ K 8
   ♣ A 8 7 6 4

S
   ♠ 10 3
   ♡ A K Q 8 7 2
   ◇ A 10 7
   ♣ J 9

West leads ♣ 10.   Trumps split 3-1.   Plan the play.

81. You are South, declarer in four spades with no
    opposition bidding.

N
   ♠ 10 9 5 3
   ♡ A Q
   ◇ 10 8 7
   ♣ K J 10 8

S
   ♠ K Q J 8 6
   ♡ 7 3
   ◇ A K 5
   ♣ 9 6 3

West leads ♡4.   Plan the play.

82. You are South, declarer in six no-trump with no opposition bidding.

N
♠ A K J
♡ A 9 5 4
♢ A Q 7
♣ A Q 4

S
♠ 7 6 5
♡ K J 6 2
♢ K 6 5
♣ K J 2

West leads ♢J. Plan the play.

83. You are South, declarer in three no-trump with no opposition bidding.

N
♠ A 10 5 3
♡ A 4 3
♢ K Q 7 4
♣ A Q

S
♠ Q J 4
♡ 10 5
♢ A 9 2
♣ J 10 9 7 6

West leads ♡2. East wins with ♡K and returns ♡6. Plan the play.

84. You are South, declarer in three no-trump with no opposition bidding.

N
♠ A Q
♡ 9 7 6
♢ Q J 10 3 2
♣ A 10 6

S
♠ K J
♡ K Q 2
♢ 9 6 4
♣ K Q 9 8 4

West leads ♠5. Plan the play.

85. You are South, declarer in three no-trump with no opposition bidding

     N   ♠ 6 4
                           ♡ K Q 6
                           ◇ 9 8 6 5 4
                           ♣ 10 3 2

     S   ♠ A 9 5
                           ♡ A 7 5
                           ◇ A Q 10 2
                           ♣ A K 9

     West leads ♠Q to which East follows with ♠8. Assuming you hold up, West continues with ♠3 to East's ♠K. Plan the play.

86. You are South, declarer in three no-trump with no opposition bidding

     N   ♠ Q 10 7
                           ♡ 2
                           ◇ A J 5
                           ♣ A Q 8 4 3 2

     S   ♠ K J 6
                           ♡ A 10 5
                           ◇ K 7 6 4 2
                           ♣ K 5

     West leads ♡4 and East plays ♡Q. Plan the play.

87. You are South with both sides vulnerable. East dealt and opened with a strong one no-trump (16-18 points) but you are declarer in four hearts.

     N   ♠ K 6 4
                           ♡ 10 9 8
                           ◇ K J 9
                           ♣ A 7 6 3

     S   ♠ 7 5
                           ♡ A Q J 7 6 4
                           ◇ A 6 3
                           ♣ J 4

     West leads ♠J which wins and continues with ♠10, taken by East with ♠Q. East next plays ♠A. Plan the play.

88. You are South, declarer in three no-trump, East having
    opened with one diamond.

    N   ♠ A J 4
                    ♡ A Q 7
                    ◇ 6 4 2
                    ♣ A 10 5 2

    S   ♠ Q 7 2
                    ♡ J 6 3
                    ◇ A 8 7
                    ♣ K Q J 9

    West leads ◇5 and East's ◇9 wins. East returns ◇K and
    you win with ◇A, West playing ◇3. West holds five small
    clubs. Plan the play.

89. You are South, declarer in four spades, West having
    overcalled one spade with two clubs.

    N   ♠ 8 6 5 3
                    ♡ 10 8 3
                    ◇ A J 4
                    ♣ A 7 2

    S   ♠ A K Q J 9
                    ♡ K J 9 4
                    ◇ 10 5 3
                    ♣ J

    West leads ♣K. Trumps are divided 3-1. Plan the play.

90. You are South, declarer in four spades after this bidding with North dealer.

S	W	N	E
		—	1♣
1♠	2♢	3♠	—
4♠	—	—	—

N   ♠8 6 4 3
            ♡A J 8 5
            ♢K Q 6
            ♣7 4

S   ♠A Q 10 7 5
            ♡6
            ♢7 4
            ♣K Q J 3 2

West leads ♣9 taken by East who returns ♢3. West wins and returns a low diamond, ruffed by East with ♠2. East returns a club, taken by South. Dummy is entered with ♡A and ♠3 is led from the table, East following with ♠9. How do you plan the play?

Answers

61. There are four top losers – three aces and the third heart. It is impossible to avoid losing the three aces so it is essential to discard a heart. There are two possibilities: (1) Win in hand and play ♣K with a view to discarding a heart on the third round of clubs. (2) Win in dummy and play ◇6, hoping East holds ◇A so that a heart can be discarded from dummy on ◇K.

Both these plans have to be put into operation before drawing trumps as the opponents will establish their heart winner before you can get your discard.

The best line is (2), that is to win in dummy and play ◇ 6 as the position of ◇ A is 50%. To get a discard on the third club requires a 3-3 split which is about 36%. A very little higher as there is a faint chance of one opponent holding a doubleton club and a singleton ace of trumps.

The full hands were

```
              ♠ J 8 7 2
              ♡ A 6 5
              ◇ 6
              ♣ Q J 10 6 5
  ♠ 4 3                      ♠ A 5
  ♡ Q J 10 2                 ♡ 9 8 3
  ◇ Q 9 5 3 2                ◇ A J 10 4
  ♣ A 7                      ♣ 9 8 3 2
              ♠ K Q 10 9 6
              ♡ K 7 4
              ◇ K 8 7
              ♣ K 4
```

10

c/f **10**

	MAX. AWARD	YOUR SCORE
b/f	**10**	

If you played clubs before touching trumps score 5 points.

62. There are eight top tricks and it is merely a question of making one more from diamonds. The safety play is to lead low to the ace and return ◇2. This will guarantee two tricks against any distribution of the remaining five.

> The full hands were:

	♠ A 6 4	
	♡ K 8 2	
	◇ A 10 4 2	
	♣ 7 4 3	
♠ 10 2		♠ Q J 8 5 3
♡ J 9 7 3		♡ 10 5 4
◇ K 9 8 6		◇ Q
♣ Q 10 2		♣ J 9 8 5
	♠ K 9 7	
	♡ A Q 6	
	◇ J 7 5 3	
	♣ A K 6	

63. Assuming the spades provide five tricks, there are twelve on top. The best chance of making one more is by reverse dummy, using dummy's K Q J to draw the adverse trumps and ruffing three clubs in hand. This requires a 3-2 trump break.

> If trumps are divided 4-1 against you the contract may be made on a squeeze. The hand was originally played by the American master, Howard Schenken in the 1951 World Championship in Naples and the full deal was:

The MAX. AWARD for question 62 is **10**.

	c/f	**20**

	MAX. AWARD	YOUR SCORE
b/f	20	

♠ J 9
♡ A 9 7 3
◇ K Q J
♣ A J 6 3

♠ 8 2   ♠ 10 7 5 4
♡ K 5 2   ♡ J 10 6 4
◇ 9 6 4   ◇ 7 2
♣ K Q 8 7 4   ♣ 10 5 2

♠ A K Q 6 3
♡ Q 8
◇ A 10 8 5 3
♣ 9

Schenken gave himself every chance. He won the opening lead with ♣A and ruffed ♣3 with ◇3. He crossed to dummy with ◇J and cashed ◇K to test the trump distribution. When both opponents followed he ruffed ♣6 with ◇10, crossed to dummy with ♠J and ruffed ♣J with ◇A. Dummy was re-entered with ♡A and the last trump was drawn with ◇Q, South discarding ♡Q. South's remaining spades provided the rest of the tricks.

If trumps are 4-1 the reverse dummy plan is abandoned. Trumps are drawn and spades cashed. On the last spade West holds ♡ K 2 and ♣Q and dummy ♡ A 9 and ♣J. Playing reverse dummy and testing trump division, score 10 points. Playing reverse dummy but not testing trump division, score 7 points.

		10

64. Win with ♣A and draw two rounds of trumps, following by ◇5 to ◇A, ◇2 to ◇Q and ◇6 finessing ◇10 unless ◇J appeared. Discard ♣4 on ◇K and ruff a club.

In your near hopeless contract your only hope is to discard dummy's low club on the fourth diamond. This requires that the

		10
c/f	40	

	MAX. AWARD	YOUR SCORE
b/f	40	

diamonds are 4-2 and trumps 3-2 and that the player with the doubleton diamond does not have the remaining trump. This is essential, for if diamonds break 3-3 it will not be possible to cash the thirteenth diamond without one opponent ruffing.

When you are in a desperate contract you must assume that the cards are distributed in the way that makes the contract possible to achieve. The full deal was:

```
              ♠ A J 6 5 4
              ♡ K J 9
              ◇ Q 6 5
              ♣ A 4
♠ K 10 8 3                  ♠ Q 9
♡ 5 4                       ♡ 6 3 2
◇ 8 3                       ◇ J 9 7 4
♣ Q J 10 7 5                ♣ K 8 6 3
              ♠ 7 2
              ♡ A Q 10 8 7
              ◇ A K 10 2
              ♣ 9 2
```

65. With a loser in hearts you can only afford to lose two trumps. Ruff the opening lead and play ♠K.

If adverse spades are 2-2 it does not matter what you do. If they are 4-0 you have no hope. If they are 3-1 a low spade gains if the distribution is A   Q J X

But ♠K gains if the distribution is either J   A Q X   or   Q   A J X

	MAX. AWARD	YOUR SCORE
	10	
c/f	50	

	MAX. AWARD	YOUR SCORE
b/f	50	

Therefore the play of ♠K is the best chance. The full hand was:

```
              ♠ –
              ♡ Q 7 4 2
              ◇ K Q 6 5 2
              ♣ J 9 5 4
♠ J                        ♠ A Q 6
♡ A J 9 6 5                ♡ K 10 8
◇ J 10 8                   ◇ 9 4
♣ K Q 10 8                 ♣ A 7 6 3 2
              ♠ K 10 9 8 7 5 4 3 2
              ♡ 3
              ◇ A 7 3
              ♣ –
```

66. (a) Hold up ♠A until third round. Cross to dummy with either ace and lead a low diamond. Assuming East plays low, win with ◇A and return to dummy with the other ace and play a diamond. If East plays ◇Q let him win. If East plays low, win with ◇K and play a third round, hoping that East has ◇J. Avoidance play. It would be wrong to play ◇A or ◇K from hand as East would (or should) unblock by playing ◇Q. By leading the suit from the table East cannot unblock. This plan only fails if West has ◇ Q X X in which case you are doomed if West also started with five spades.

(b) Yes. You should win the second spade with ♠A and play as before. If East has a third spade the suit is split 4-3 and you can only lose three spade tricks. If you hold up ♠A until the third round, East has a chance to discard ◇Q to create an entry for his partner with ◇J.

	5	
	5	
c/f	60	

	MAX. AWARD	YOUR SCORE
b/f	**60**	

Full hand:

```
            ♠ 5 2
            ♡ A 8 4 3
            ◇ 7 6 2
            ♣ A 8 7 3
♠ K Q J 10 8              ♠ 9 4 3
♡ Q J 6                  ♡ 10 9 7
◇ J 10 9                 ◇ Q 8
♣ 4 2                    ♣ Q J 10 9 5
            ♠ A 7 6
            ♡ K 5 2
            ◇ A K 5 4 3
            ♣ K 6
```

67. Win with ♡A and lead a low diamond. West wins with ◇K and his next lead is immaterial. Assume he plays clubs, South wins and leads to ◇Q and plays a trump. East ducks and South wins with ♠10, West discarding. Dummy is entered by ruffing ◇A for another trump lead.

The only danger to the contract is a 4-0 trump break and this can only be managed if the ace is on the right and it is possible to lead twice from the table. This proved to be necessary as the four hands were:

```
            ♠ 7 4 3
            ♡ J 8 6 3
            ◇ Q J
            ♣ 10 7 5 3
♠ –                      ♠ A K 9 8
♡ K Q 10 9              ♡ 7 5 4 2
◇ K 8 7 5 4             ◇ 10 9 6
♣ 9 8 4 2               ♣ J 6
            ♠ Q J 10 6 5 2
            ♡ A
            ◇ A 3 2
            ♣ A K Q
```

	10	

| **c/f** | **70** | |

	MAX. AWARD	YOUR SCORE
b/f	70	

68. Win with ◇K, draw trumps, eliminate clubs and diamonds by ruffing the third round. Either lead a low spade from hand or a low spade from dummy and duck.

    There appear to be two spade losers, but valuable inferences are available from the bidding and opening lead. West is likely to hold a five card spade suit for his overcall and he is unlikely to have ♠ K Q J, having failed to lead ♠K. Therefore East has a singleton honour. By playing as recommended, if West ducks a spade from hand, East must win and concede a ruff and discard. If West wins with ♠K, felling East's ♠Q (or ♠J) he must lead from his remaining honour into ♠ A 10 or give a ruff and discard.

    The full deal was:

	♠ 7 6 3 2	
	♡ A Q 8 6	
	◇ 8 4	
	♣ A 9 6	

♠ K J 9 8 4		♠ Q
♡ 3 2		♡ 7 4
◇ Q J 10		◇ 9 7 4 3 2
♣ Q 10 5		♣ J 8 4 3 2

	♠ A 10 5	
	♡ K J 10 9 5	
	◇ A K 6	
	♣ K 7	

MAX. AWARD: 10

69. Win with ♣K, cross to dummy with ♡A and lead ◇2. If East ducks and ◇Q wins, switch to spades making three spades, three hearts, one diamond and two clubs.

    If East holds ◇A and plays it on the first round he gives you four tricks in diamonds. If he ducks you have time to establish spades. If West holds ◇A he cannot profitably continue clubs.

MAX. AWARD: 10

| c/f | 90 | |

	MAX. AWARD	YOUR SCORE
b/f	90	

Full deal:

```
              ♠ Q J 4 2
              ♡ A K 6
              ◇ K J 7 6 2
              ♣ 5
♠ A 8 6 3                    ♠ 9 7
♡ 9 8                        ♡ J 10 5 4
◇ 8                          ◇ A 10 9 4
♣ Q 9 8 6 4 3                ♣ J 7 2
              ♠ K 10 5
              ♡ Q 7 3 2
              ◇ Q 5 3
              ♣ A K 10
```

As it happens you will succeed if you play spades at trick two, but this is fortuitous as West holds ♠A. If East holds ♠A and returns a club you will not have enough tricks unless the hearts are 3-3. If West holds ◇A, you are down. Playing a low diamond from dummy at trick three virtually guarantees the contract regardless of the position of ◇A and ♠A.

70. Hold up ♠A until third round and lead ◇2. If West plays ◇Q let it hold. If West plays low win with ◇K and return to ◇A. Re-enter dummy with either ace and clear diamonds. This play only fails if East has ◇ Q X X. To play ◇A from hand risks losing to East's ◇J on the third round.

	MAX. AWARD	YOUR SCORE
	10	
c/f	100	

	MAX. AWARD	YOUR SCORE
b/f	100	

The four hands were:

```
              ♠ 6 5
              ♡ A 10 7
              ◇ K 10 8 7 6 5 3
              ♣ A
♠ J 8 4                      ♠ K Q 9 7 3
♡ J 8 6 5 4                  ♡ Q 2
◇ Q                          ◇ J 9 4
♣ 10 9 7 2                   ♣ Q J 4
              ♠ A 10 2
              ♡ K 9 3
              ◇ A 2
              ♣ K 8 6 5 3
```

71. Ruff with ♠8 or higher and draw trumps. Lead a low diamond to the ace to guard against ◇J 10 X X with East. If West discards on the first round return ◇2 from table and cover East's card. Assuming he plays an honour, return to dummy with ♠6 to play diamonds again.

10

Full deal was:

```
              ♠ 6 3 2
              ♡ K J 8
              ◇ A 7 4 2
              ♣ K J 5
♠ 10 7                       ♠ 5
♡ 9 6 5 4 3                  ♡ A Q 10 7 2
◇ –                          ◇ J 10 5 3
♣ A Q 10 7 6 2               ♣ 9 8 3
              ♠ A K Q J 9 8 4
              ♡ –
              ◇ K Q 9 8 6
              ♣ 4
```

Although East-West have a cheap save in hearts it is not easy for either to enter the bidding at the score.

c/f	110	

	MAX. AWARD	YOUR SCORE
b/f	**110**	

72. Duck ♠Q and win the return. Play three rounds only of diamonds ending in dummy. Exit with a spade. West can cash three spades and you will discard ♡ 6 4 from dummy and ♡2 and ♣2 from hand. West must lead either a heart or club, in either case giving you an extra trick.

    The four hands were:

```
                    ♠ 10 8 3
                    ♡ 10 6 4
                    ◇ Q J 8 6
                    ♣ A 7 5
    ♠ K J 6 5 4                  ♠ Q 2
    ♡ K 3                        ♡ J 9 8 7 5
    ◇ 10 4 3                     ◇ 9 7 5
    ♣ Q 10 9                     ♣ 8 4 3
                    ♠ A 9 7
                    ♡ A Q 2
                    ◇ A K 2
                    ♣ K J 6 2
```

If South cashes the fourth diamond early he will be unable to discard safely on the last spade.

	10	

73. Duck the opening lead and win the probable continuation of ◇J with ◇K. Draw trumps, cash ◇A and lead ♣4 to ♣Q. Assuming this wins, cash ♣A and exit with a third club. West wins and must lead a spade or give a ruff and discard.

    It is tempting to try to end play West with the third diamond but there is no guarantee that he will have to win it. But ♣K must surely be with West on his double. He must have all the remaining high cards. West might unblock his ♣K under ♣A, trusting his partner for ♣J – just possible. But this would not help the defence, nor give an overtrick as South would then lose two spades. West would have done

	10	

c/f	**130**	

	MAX. AWARD	YOUR SCORE
b/f	**130**	

better to have led a trump and it would have been difficult to eliminate the diamonds without East getting in.

The full hand was:

```
              ♠ 7 3 2
              ♡ Q 10 3 2
              ◇ K 4 2
              ♣ A Q 3
♠ A Q J 8                  ♠ 10 9 6 5
♡ 7 4                      ♡ 9 6
◇ Q J 9 3                  ◇ 10 8 7
♣ K 10 2                   ♣ 9 8 6 5
              ♠ K 4
              ♡ A K J 8 5
              ◇ A 6 5
              ♣ J 7 4
```

74. Ruff opening lead and cash ♡ K Q. If East discards on second trump, play ♣K followed by ♣4. If West ruffs he ruffs a loser. If he discards, win with ♣A and play a third round. You can now ruff a fourth club in dummy with ♡A. If West had a singleton trump you play ♣4 to ♣A and return ♣3 so that East cannot ruff a winner.

The full deal was:

```
              ♠ K 8 6
              ♡ A 9 4
              ◇ K 8 5 3
              ♣ A 7 3
♠ Q 10 4 3                 ♠ 9 7 5 2
♡ 10 3 2                   ♡ 6
◇ Q J 10 9 2               ◇ A 7 6 4
♣ Q                        ♣ J 10 9 2
              ♠ A J
              ♡ K Q J 8 7 5
              ◇ –
              ♣ K 8 6 5 4
```

10

c/f	**140**	

	MAX. AWARD	YOUR SCORE
b/f	**140**	
	10	
c/f	**150**	

If trumps are 2-2 or clubs 3-2 the contract is lay down. It is necessary however to guard against trumps being 3-1 and clubs 4-1.

75. Win in hand and lead a low spade. East wins with ♠K and returns a club. Win and lead a low spade.

This hand was played by the late Helen Sobel in the U.S. National Pairs Championship 1948. North was Margaret Wagar.

The full deal was:

```
                ♠ 8 5
                ♡ 10 7 4 2
                ♢ A 9 6 3
                ♣ K 5 4
    ♠ 10 9 4 2              ♠ A K
    ♡ 3                     ♡ K J 9 8 6
    ♢ Q 8 5 4               ♢ 10 2
    ♣ 10 8 7 2              ♣ J 9 6 3
                ♠ Q J 7 6 3
                ♡ A Q 5
                ♢ K J 7
                ♣ A Q
```

When West led ♣2 Helen Sobel reasoned that West must have a singleton heart and was trying another suit. As she held only four clubs her shape must be 4-1-4-4. East on the opening bid must have practically all the missing points including ♠ A K. Therefore it was logical to play low spades each time as ♠ A K must be doubleton. South made three spades, two hearts, three clubs and two diamonds for an overtrick.

	MAX. AWARD	YOUR SCORE
b/f	**150**	

76. Win in hand, cross to ♠K or ♠A and lead ♣8.   **10**

After the lead South has six top tricks. He can make nine if clubs break 3-3 or if he can make all his diamonds. But there is not time to establish more than one suit. The only high card that can be placed with reasonable confidence is ♣A which must surely be with East on his double. By playing a low club from the table success is assured. If East plays ♣A South had three club tricks. If East ducks, South has time to establish diamonds. The hand arose in an inter-county match and the full deal was:

```
              ♠ A K 8 6 4
              ♡ 9 5
              ◇ J 6 5
              ♣ K Q 8
  ♠ 3 2                      ♠ Q 9 7 5
  ♡ J 10 7 6 4              ♡ K 8 3 2
  ◇ Q 7 4 2                 ◇ 3
  ♣ 7 6                     ♣ A 10 9 5
              ♠ J 10
              ♡ A Q
              ◇ A K 10 9 8
              ♣ J 4 3 2
```

77. Win with ♡A and lead ♠K. East wins, cashes ♡K and exits with a trump, all following, Lead ◇3 to ◇A. Return to hand with a trump and lead a low diamond.   **10**

This hand was played by Michael O'Connell in the Irish C.B.A teams championship in 1963.

The normal play would be to finesse diamonds. If this failed the suit might split 3-3, failing which the club finesse might be right.

O'Connell's line of play is superior. If the diamond finesse were to be right (i.e. ◇K with West), by playing twice towards dummy's ◇ Q J,

c/f	**170**	

	MAX. AWARD	YOUR SCORE
b/f	170	

using ♣A as the second entry, South's ♣2 can be discarded on a diamond winner. If East has ◊K the contract is made if he has ◊K, ◊ K X, ◊ K X X. In the actual lay out he is end-played as he must either lead a club into the tenace, or a heart giving a ruff and discard. Only if East has ◊ K 9 X X or better is there a problem. In that event the club finesse is still available and as West will be known to hold more clubs than East, East having at least five hearts and four diamonds, the probability is that ♣Q is with West.

The full deal was:

```
              ♠ K 8 6 2
              ♡ A 2
              ◊ A Q J 2
              ♣ K J 5
♠ 7 5                        ♠ A 4
♡ Q J 10 5                   ♡ K 8 7 4 3
◊ 10 9 7 4                   ◊ K 5
♣ 10 7 4                     ♣ Q 9 8 3
              ♠ Q J 10 9 3
              ♡ 9 6
              ◊ 8 6 3
              ♣ A 6 2
```

This hand was originally contributed by the late Jack Kelly to "Bridge Writer's Choice", comprising hands from members of the International Bridge Press Association.

78. Play ♣ A J 5. If all follow (i.e. clubs 3-3) play three rounds of hearts, discarding a diamond, and follow with ♣K to discard last diamond. If East discards on the third round of clubs, play the fourth club before touching hearts. In any event play clubs before hearts.

The problem is to discard two diamonds

	10	
c/f	180	

	MAX. AWARD	YOUR SCORE
b/f	180	

before the opponents ruff. Irrespective of whether or not hearts go round three times, the contract is impossible unless West has at least three clubs. For this reason clubs must be played first and if West ruffs early the contract was doomed from the start. In fact the four hands were:

♠ J 7 5 2
♡ A Q 5
◇ Q 3
♣ K Q 10 4

♠ Q 10 8   ♠ 9
♡ 10 8   ♡ J 9 7 4 3 2
◇ J 10 9 4   ◇ K 8 7 2
♣ 9 7 6 2   ♣ 8 3

♠ A K 6 4 3
♡ K 6
◇ A 6 5
♣ A J 5

79. Win with ◇A and lead ♠3 and finesse if East follows low. It appears odd to finesse against a queen with ten combined trumps including ace and king, but it is a safety play.

If East has ♠ Q X X South makes seven trumps plus two hearts and a diamond. If West takes ♠10 with ♠Q the trumps split 2-1 and there will be an entry to dummy with ♠6. This will enable South to set up a club winner for his losing heart.

	MAX. AWARD	YOUR SCORE
	10	

	MAX. AWARD	YOUR SCORE
c/f	190	

	MAX. AWARD	YOUR SCORE
b/f	**190**	

Full deal:

```
                    ♠ 6 5 3
                    ♡ 9 8 6
                    ◇ A 3 2
                    ♣ Q J 8 7
♠ –                                    ♠ Q 8 2
♡ J 7 5 2                              ♡ Q 10 3
◇ K Q 10 9 8                           ◇ J 7 5 4
♣ A K 10 9                             ♣ 5 4 2
                    ♠ A K J 10 9 7 4
                    ♡ A K 4
                    ◇ 6
                    ♣ 6 3
```

80. Win with ♣A and draw trumps. Lead ♣J. East wins and probably returns a spade. If West discards on the second club you can easily ruff out East's club honour. If West followed to the second club you can afford to ruff a third club in hand as you only need to establish one extra trick, a long club.

It is tempting to ruff a diamond on the table as this appears relatively safe with only five between you. This is the line adopted by declarer in an inter-club match and he was over-ruffed for one down. If you also tried to ruff a diamond score 5 points as it is a bit unlucky to lose.

		10	

	MAX. AWARD	YOUR SCORE
c/f	**200**	

	MAX. AWARD	YOUR SCORE
b/f	**200**	

The full deal was:

　　　　　♠ A K 5
　　　　　♡ 6 5 3
　　　　　◇ K 8
　　　　　♣ A 8 7 6 4

♠ 9 8 7 6 4　　　　　　　♠ Q J 3
♡ 10　　　　　　　　　　♡ J 9 4
◇ Q J 6 4 3 2　　　　　　◇ 9 5
♣ 10　　　　　　　　　　♣ K Q 5 3 2

　　　　　♠ 10 3
　　　　　♡ A K Q 8 7 2
　　　　　◇ A 10 7
　　　　　♣ J 9

81. Win with ♡A and play trumps. Later finesse West for ♣Q. You might have as many as five losers and the key card is ♣Q. If this is with West you can make the contract. If East has ♣Q you are down even if the heart finesse wins. Consider the full deal:

　　　　　♠ 10 9 5 3
　　　　　♡ A Q
　　　　　◇ 10 8 7
　　　　　♣ K J 10 8

♠ A 7　　　　　　　　　♠ 4 2
♡ J 9 6 4　　　　　　　♡ K 10 8 5 2
◇ J 9 6 2　　　　　　　◇ Q 4 3
♣ Q 7 4　　　　　　　　♣ A 5 2

　　　　　♠ K Q J 8 6
　　　　　♡ 7 3
　　　　　◇ A K 5
　　　　　♣ 9 6 3

You win with ♡A and lose a trump to West. After cashing ♡K a diamond is returned which you win, draw trumps and lead ♣3 to ♣10, losing to ♣A. Take the diamond return and lead ♣9 taking the marked finesse, and discard ◇5 on the

| **c/f** | **210** | |

	MAX. AWARD	YOUR SCORE
c/f	210	

fourth club. Suppose you finesse hearts at trick one and lose. Opponents have the three entries needed to set up a diamond (♡K, ♠A and ♣A). By winning with ♡A they have only two effective entries as ♠A and ♡K no longer represent two separate entries.

Finally, if West has ♡K and East ♣Q, you are down even if you finesse ♡Q at trick one. The defence return a diamond when in with ♠A and another when in with ♣Q and cash their winner when in with ♣A.

82. Win in hand and finesse ♠J. Then:

(1) If ♠J holds make the safety play in hearts, leading ♡4 to ♡K, returning ♡2 and covering West's card. If he plays low insert ♡9 and this ensures three tricks on any distribution. If West shows out on the second round, play ♡A and lead back towards ♡J 6.

(2) If ♠J loses to ♠Q you need all four heart tricks and cannot afford any safety play. Therefore play ♡4 from the table and finesse ♡J. The first round finesse is correct. East must hold ♡Q for your contract to win. If hearts are 3-2 all is well. If East has singleton ♡Q you can finesse against West's ♡10 with ♡ A 9 in dummy. This will not be possible if you lead ♡A. If West has singleton ♡Q you cannot avoid a loser to East with ♡ 10 8 7 3.

	10	

	MAX. AWARD	YOUR SCORE
b/f	220	

	MAX. AWARD	YOUR SCORE
b/f	**220**	

The full deal was in fact:

```
              ♠ A K J
              ♡ A 9 5 4
              ◇ A Q 7
              ♣ A Q 4
♠ Q 3 2                    ♠ 10 9 8 4
♡ Q 10 7 3                 ♡ 8
◇ J 10 9                   ◇ 8 4 3 2
♣ 10 9 5                   ♣ 8 7 6 3
              ♠ 7 6 5
              ♡ K J 6 2
              ◇ K 6 5
              ♣ K J 2
```

83. Win the second heart as the suit appears to be
   4-4. Lead ♣Q from dummy. If ♣Q is taken
   opponents can cash three hearts but you will
   make four clubs, three diamonds, one spade
   and one heart. If ♣Q is ducked, cross to hand
   with ◇A and lead ♠Q. You then make three or
   four spades, one heart, two clubs and three or
   four diamonds.

   If you play ♣A and ♣Q and opponents hold
   off you are short of entries to employ the clubs.
   You cannot afford to give a spade as you will
   lose three hearts, one club and one spade.

   The hand was originally played by Canadian
   international, Eric Murray.

		10

	MAX. AWARD	YOUR SCORE
c/f	**230**	

	MAX. AWARD	YOUR SCORE
b/f	230	

```
              ♠ A 10 5 3
              ♡ A 4 3
              ◇ K Q 7 4
              ♣ A Q
♠ 9 8                      ♠ K 7 6 2
♡ Q J 8 2                  ♡ K 9 7 6
◇ J 10 8 3                 ◇ 6 5
♣ K 4 3                    ♣ 8 5 2
              ♠ Q J 4
              ♡ 10 5
              ◇ A 9 2
              ♣ J 10 9 7 6
```

84. Win in dummy and lead a heart. Assuming ♡K wins lead ♣K and unblock ♣10 from the table. Next lead ♣4 to ♣A. If West shows out (as in fact he does) you have a marked finesse against East's ♣ J X. Then play ♡7. If East ducks and ♡Q wins, cross to dummy with ♠A and lead ♣6, finessing. The need to unblock ♣10 is now apparent, as you would be unable to get back to hand without overtaking ♣10 and later losing to ♣J.

The full deal:

```
              ♠ A Q
              ♡ 9 7 6
              ◇ Q J 10 3 2
              ♣ A 10 6
♠ 10 8 6 5 3              ♠ 9 7 4 2
♡ J 10 8 3               ♡ A 5 4
◇ K 8 5                  ◇ A 7
♣ 3                      ♣ J 7 5 2
              ♠ K J
              ♡ K Q 2
              ◇ 9 6 4
              ♣ K Q 9 8 4
```

		10

	MAX. AWARD	YOUR SCORE
c/f	240	

	MAX. AWARD	YOUR SCORE
b/f	**240**	

Clearly you cannot attempt to clear diamonds as you have no time.

If you played a heart at trick two, ♣K at trick three but failed to unblock ♣10 score 5 points.

85. Hold up to third round. Cross to dummy with ♡Q (or ♡K) and lead a low diamond. If East plays low put up ◇A.

10

If West holds a five card spade suit (no worry if 4-4) and has guarded ◇K you are down. The only way in which West might get in when it could be prevented is with singleton ◇K. If East has ◇K it does not matter.

Full deal:

```
              ♠ 6 4
              ♡ K Q 6
              ◇ 9 8 6 5 4
              ♣ 10 3 2
♠ Q J 10 7 3              ♠ K 8 2
♡ J 9 8                  ♡ 10 4 3 2
◇ K                      ◇ J 7 3
♣ 8 6 5 4                ♣ Q J 7
              ♠ A 9 5
              ♡ A 7 5
              ◇ A Q 10 2
              ♣ A K 9
```

It would be wrong to play ◇A from hand. If East held ◇K alone, West would have an entry with ◇J. If you lead diamonds from dummy and ◇K appears from East, let him hold it. If you played ◇A from hand you score 5 points.

86. Win with ♡A. There is little point in holding up as West cannot have more than five hearts on his lead. Play ♣5 to ♣A (or ♣Q) and return ♣2 to ♣K. If all follow you have nine tricks for certain. If the clubs do not break you will need

| c/f | **250** | |

	MAX. AWARD	YOUR SCORE
b/f	250	

five tricks from diamonds and this will not be possible unless you are in your hand to lead towards ◇ A J 5 and finesse.

| | 10 | |

When the hand was originally played in a team match the clubs broke badly but the diamonds were favourable.

```
                    ♠ Q 10 7
                    ♡ 2
                    ◇ A J 5
                    ♣ A Q 8 4 3 2
    ♠ A 8 5 3                      ♠ 9 4 2
    ♡ K J 8 4 3                    ♡ Q 9 7 6
    ◇ Q 10 3                       ◇ 9 8
    ♣ 6                            ♣ J 10 9 7
                    ♠ K J 6
                    ♡ A 10 5
                    ◇ K 7 6 4 2
                    ♣ K 5
```

87. Discard a diamond on third spade. If East returns ♣K or ♣Q win with ♣A and finesse trumps. Play out the rest of the trumps, discarding clubs from the table. East must have all the remaining high cards and will be squeezed on the last trump, having to discard from ◇ Q X X and ♣Q. If East continues with a fourth spade instead of a club, ruff in the closed hand in case East held ♡ K X X X.

An alternative plan, not quite so good, is to ruff the third spade, cross to dummy with ♣A and finesse trumps, leaving dummy with ◇ K J 9. When you lead out trumps East will have to discard twice from ◇ Q X X and ♣ K Q X. If he discards clubs put him in with the last club to play into diamonds. If he releases a diamond, play ◇A and ◇K and fell his ◇Q. This plan might fail if East false-carded, leaving himself with ◇ Q X and ♣ K 10 instead of ◇ Q X X

| | 10 | |
| c/f | 270 | |

	MAX. AWARD	YOUR SCORE
b/f	**270**	

and ♣Q. For this line of plan score 7 points.

A third line is to lead ◇J from the table with a view to a backward finesse against ◇10. But East may well have ◇ Q 10 X. Score 3 points.

The full deal was:

```
              ♠ K 6 4
              ♡ 10 9 8
              ◇ K J 9
              ♣ A 7 6 3
  ♠ J 10 9 3 2              ♠ A Q 8
  ♡ 2                       ♡ K 5 3
  ◇ 8 7 5 2                 ◇ Q 10 4
  ♣ 9 5 2                   ♣ K Q 10 8
              ♠ 7 5
              ♡ A Q J 7 6 4
              ◇ A 6 3
              ♣ J 4
```

88. Cash ♣A. Assume East discards a spade. Exit with a diamond. On East's winners dummy discards ♣ 5 2 and South ♠2 and ♡3. East must now lead from one of his kings. Suppose he plays a heart. Win with ♡J, lead ♠7 to ♠A (Vienna Coup) and cash the remaining clubs, discarding ♠ J 4 from the table. On the last club East is squeezed, having either to throw ♠K or unguard hearts. If East returns a spade at trick seven instead of a heart, win with ♠Q, cross to ♡A and play as before. If East declines to cash his diamonds he will be unable to find safe discards on the clubs.

This hand originally appeared in a Par Contest at Blackpool in 1960 and the four hands were:

	10	

c/f	**280**	

	MAX. AWARD	YOUR SCORE
b/f	**280**	

```
                    ♠ A J 4
                    ♡ A Q 7
                    ◇ 6 4 2
                    ♣ A 10 5 2
    ♠ 10 9 3                      ♠ K 8 6 5
    ♡ 9 8 4                       ♡ K 10 5 2
    ◇ 5 3                         ◇ K Q J 10 9
    ♣ 8 7 6 4 3                   ♣ —
                    ♠ Q 7 2
                    ♡ J 6 3
                    ◇ A 8 7
                    ♣ K Q J 9
```

89. Win with ♣A and draw trumps. Lead a low
    heart from hand. If West wins with ♡Q and
    switches to a diamond play low from the table.
    Assume East wins, he cannot safely return the
    suit and probably returns a club. You ruff and
    play another heart. You can now discard the
    third diamond in dummy on the fourth heart. If
    East wins the first heart lead, he cannot play
    diamonds without giving you an extra trick. To
    attempt to play hearts before tackling trumps
    risks a ruff.   **10**
       Full deal:

```
                    ♠ 8 6 5 3
                    ♡ 10 8 3
                    ◇ A J 4
                    ♣ A 7 2
    ♠ 2                            ♠ 10 7 4
    ♡ A Q 6 5                      ♡ 7 2
    ◇ 7 5                          ◇ K Q 9 8 2
    ♣ K Q 10 9 8 6                 ♣ 5 4 3
                    ♠ A K Q J 9
                    ♡ K J 9 4
                    ◇ 10 6 3
                    ♣ J
```

| c/f | **290** | |

	MAX. AWARD	YOUR SCORE
b/f	290	

90. Finesse ♠10. East has shown up with four clubs and one diamond. He opened one club and his distribution must be 4-4-1-4.

This problem originally appeared in a B.B.C. radio series in 1965 and published in *Best of Bridge on the Air*.

The full deal was:

		10

```
              ♠ 8 6 4 3
              ♡ A J 8 5
              ◇ K Q 6
              ♣ 7 4
♠ –                          ♠ K J 9 2
♡ 10 9 7 3                   ♡ K Q 4 2
◇ A J 10 9 8 5 2             ◇ 3
♣ 9 5                       ♣ A 10 8 6
              ♠ A Q 10 7 5
              ♡ 6
              ◇ 7 4
              ♣ K Q J 3 2
```

| **Total** | 300 | |

Rate Your Declarer Play

	Max 300
Excellent. You can well afford to bid boldly.	250-300
Above average. You will not lose many contracts that are there.	150-200
Considerable scope for improvement – perhaps defence is your *forte*?	150-below

THE DAILY TELEGRAPH BOOK OF BRIDGE

G.C.H. Fox

"The ideal bedside book."

Rixi Markus, *Guardian*

"Both instructive and entertaining."

Derek Rimington, *Harrow Observer*

HOW TO READ YOUR OPPONENTS' CARDS

Mike Lawrence

"Mike Lawrence has written a book for those with aspirations to real expertise."

Harold Franklin, *Yorkshire Post*

"Really an excellent book on how to play the cards."

G.C.H. Fox, *Daily Telegraph*

DOUBLES

Robert B. Ewen

"A significant work ranging all the way from basic through modern and hyper-modern practice."

The Bridge World

"Ewen covers the subject from every angle. Players at all levels are likely to find this book most instructive."

G.C.H. Fox, *Daily Telegraph*

Clerkenwell House, Clerkenwell Green, London EC1

BRIDGE: Standard Bidding

G.C.H. Fox

"G.C.H. Fox is a good teacher, and those who are anxious to improve their bidding will surely find this book the answer to their needs."

E.P.C. Cotter, *The Financial Times*

"His theme is to show not merely what a player should bid but also the reason why he should bid it; and his experience as a player, writer and teacher enables him to carry out his theme with marked success."

George Hervey, *The Field*

PRE-EMPTIVE BIDDING

Robert B. Ewen

"Defense to pre-emptive bids, responding to partner's pre-emptive bids and tactics and conventions are dealt with in depth and with complete lucidity. And Ewen even gives some pointers on play after a pre-emptive bid."

Rixi Markus, *Evening Standard*

"Robert Ewen's new book is an important contribution in a specialized area of bidding which is fraught with much misunderstanding. Provides the wherewithal to find your way in one of the most confusing aspects of your bidding scheme."

George Levinrew, *Jerusalem Post*

Clerkenwell House, Clerkenwell Green, London EC1

THE EXPERT GAME

Terence Reese

"As a study of advanced techniques in the play of the cards it is unsurpassed."

Eric Milnes, *Bridge Magazine*

"The best bridge book ever written."

Pat Cotter, *Country Life*

REESE ON PLAY

"A book you cannot afford to miss."

E.P.C. Cotter, *The Financial Times*

"Revised and rewritten, it remains an outstanding book."

G.C.H. Fox, *Daily Telegraph*

THE EDUCATION OF A BRIDGE PLAYER

Howard Schenken

"A cavalcade through the great events of bridge history, a record of stirring personal experiences by one who played a leading part in them all. A book which any educated bridge player would be truly sorry to miss."

Victor Mollo, *Bridge Magazine*

"A fascinating first-hand account of the growth of bridge, and an endearing self-portrait of one of the games greatest exponents."

Albert Dormer, *IBPA Bulletin*

Clerkenwell House, Clerkenwell Green, London EC1

THE FINESSE

Fred L. Karpin

"Though intended mainly for the average player, some of the more advanced situations will intrigue even the expert."

Eric Milnes, *Bridge Magazine*

"Illustrates every facet of one of the most common plays in bridge."

Victor Mollo, *Evening Standard*

POWERHOUSE HANDS

Albert Dormer

"Should be read by everyone who aims to improve his game."

George Hervey, *The Field*

"Deals clearly and competently with every aspect of high level bidding."

Rixi Markus, *Evening Standard*

Clerkenwell House, Clerkenwell Green, London EC1

SHERLOCK HOLMES, BRIDGE DETECTIVE

Frank Thomas and George Gooden

"A most enjoyable book, giving valuable instruction and entertainment."

G.C.H. Fox, *Daily Telegraph*

"It's an original entertaining book studded with instructional hands."
Evening Standard

"Highly recommended."
Alfred Sheinwold

"The bridge instruction is excellent – although most experts will have seen some of the hands before, they are well presented and amusingly written."
Popular Bridge Monthly

"One of the biggest bridge book successes of recent time."
Don Evans, *Sydney Telegraph*

GOREN ON PLAY AND DEFENSE

"An expensive book but worth every penny to anyone who needs to improve his playing technique. The most comprehensive work on play and defence yet published."
R.A. Priday, *Sunday Telegraph*

"Excellently produced and likely to become a classic."
G.C.H. Fox, *Daily Telegraph*

Clerkenwell House, Clerkenwell Green, London EC1

"A comprehensive and authoritative study of all aspects of card play."

Rixi Markus, *Evening Standard*

"Well-organised, beautifully produced, entertaining and exhaustive."

The Bridge World

MASTER PLAY

G.C.H. Fox

"A selection of hands played by the world's greatest players. For a student of the game or for a player who wishes to browse the book is very interesting."

Derek Rimington, *Harrow Observer*

"The author gives an insight into what makes a world champion, with accounts of hands from world and European championships. An absorbing, at times dramatic, tale."

Daily Telegraph

GOREN SETTLES THE BRIDGE ARGUMENTS

"Covers practically every bidding situation in question and answer form ... should prove interesting and instructive to many players."

G.C.H. Fox, *Daily Telegraph*

Clerkenwell House, Clerkenwell Green, London EC1

"A novel method of answering knotty problems that cause frequent misunderstandings at the bridge table."

R.A. Priday, *Sunday Telegraph*

"Successfully presents a new style of instruction."

Terence Reese, *The Observer*

THE PRECISION OF BIDDING

Presented by Charles H. Goren

"No bidding system has made a greater impact since the war than the Precision system devised by C.C. Wei. Protagonists of Precision have reached the final of two world championships and won numerous prestige events throughout Europe and America. It is therefore timely that an excellent book on the system has been published.

The system has three great advantages. It is simple, it is fun to play and it is easy to add individual gadgets on to the general framework.

Goren's book outlines the development of Precision bidding, and after each opening bid gives a comprehensive and instructive quiz at the end of each chapter. There are sections on asking bids and advanced developments and a chapter showing the system in action in important championships."

R.A. Priday, *Sunday Telegraph*

"A first-class system that calls for the attention of all who take the game *au grand sérieux*."

George F. Hervey, *The Field*

Clerkenwell House, Clerkenwell Green, London EC1

"With the ever-increasing number of players showing interest in the Precision Club, I am frequently being asked for details of books on the system. The clearest exposition so far is in *The Precision System of Bidding*."

G.C.H. Fox, *Daily Telegraph*

"It must be useful to know about a system which is definitely increasing the number of its disciples steadily all over the world, and at last we have an excellent textbook on it.

The Precision Club could easily provide the answer to your ambitious dreams.

Rixi Markus, *Manchester Guardian Weekly*

"Precision is the newest and certainly one of the best of the many tournament systems which use a strong and unconditionally forcing opening bid of one club.

Precision is not for rank and file bridge players. But it is of great interest for experienced tournament partnerships which are prepared to do some study and then get plenty of practice."

Frank Cayley, *Sydney Morning Herald*

DUPLICATE BRIDGE

G.C.H. Fox

"Extensively revised, with a wealth of new material, *Duplicate Bridge*, first published nearly twenty years ago, remains to this day one of the most instructive books on the subject. Many new examples appear in the new edition illustrating every aspect of bidding and play in the light of IMPS and match point scoring."

Victor Mollo, *Evening Standard*

Clerkenwell House, Clerkenwell Green, London EC1

"Even if you are already a dedicated duplicate player, get this book."

Rhoda Lederer, E B U

"For students of duplicate and those wishing to make the transition from rubber bridge I can think of no better book. It is truly professionally written as we have come to expect from the bridge correspondent to the *Daily Telegraph*."

Derek Rimington, *Harrow Observer*

"If anyone is thinking of taking up tournament bridge for the first time, he will find *Duplicate Bridge* an invaluable guide."

E.P.C. Cotter, *Financial Times*

"Highly recommended to all serious players."

Lindsay Adams, *New Zealand Bridge*

WINNING DECLARER PLAY

Dorothy Hayden

"It is a very good book and can be strongly recommended."

G.C.H. Fox, *Daily Telegraph*

"The best book on play in twenty years."

Oswald Jacoby

Clerkenwell House, Clerkenwell Green, London EC1

HOWARD SCHENKEN'S 'BIG CLUB'

"An instructive book backed up by many interesting examples from international competition."

Sunday Telegraph

"One Club syustems are gaining general acceptance. Readers could not have a more agreeable introduction to this style from Howard Schenken's 'Big Club'."

Terence Reese, *The Observer*

OPENING LEADS

Robert B. Ewen

"Robert B. Ewen's *Opening Leads* is the first comprehensive treatment of the most important single aspect of contract bridge – a highly instructive and entertaining book which should be read by anyone who wants to improve his game."

Charles Goren

"Original and important ... bridges the gap between the average player and the expert."

Alan Truscott, *The New York Times*

"An excellent book, strongly recommended."

G.C.H. Fox, *Daily Telegraph*

Clerkenwell House, Clerkenwell Green, London EC1

SECRETS OF WINNING BRIDGE

Jeff Rubens

"This is not a book for the beginner, and even intermediate players will find parts of it difficult – the explanations are lucid and some of the concepts highly advanced. The experts who think they know it all will have to borrow a copy if they are not to fall behind the times."

Alan Truscott, The New York Times

"An excellent book for the intermediate or advanced player. There are new concepts on hand valuation tactics, and match play.

I consider this book a 'must' for one's library."

Rixi Markus, The Guardian

Clerkenwell House, Clerkenwell Green, London EC1